THE GENERATIONS MEET

Life Lessons from Our Mother's Gardens

Dr. Janice Hodges Moss

THE GENERATIONS MEET: Life Lessons from Our Mother's Gardens

Dr. Janice Moss
P. O. Box 710774
Houston, TX 77271
www.janicemoss.com

ISBN-13: 978-0-9836526-1-8
ISBN-10: 0-9836526-1-9

The interviews enclosed are printed with the permission of the interviewee.

Printed in the United States of America

Publisher's Cataloging-in-Publication

(Provided by Quality Books, Inc.)

Moss, Janice Hodges.

The generations meet : life lessons from our mother's

gardens / Janice Hodges Moss.

p. cm.

ISBN-13: 978-0-9836526-1-8

ISBN-10: 0-9836526-1-9

1. Intergenerational relations. 2. Women.

I. Title.

HM726.M67 2012   306.87

QBI12-600012

"Some of the things I know, I know only because older women have told me their secrets. I have lived and am living long so that I can tell my secrets to young women. That is the reason we women go on improving."

--Maya Angelou

Acknowledgments

To my mom, Mrs. Ludie Hodges, for the lessons and the example; I miss you every day. Thanks to my siblings: Ernstine, Johnnie, James, Nathaniel, Willie and Shirley who have loved me, supported me and encouraged me. Thanks for the love and especially the laughter.

A special thanks to Myrna Bentley, Louise Strickland, Audrey Brooks, Lois Coogle, Gertrude Sanders, Dolola Bates, Jodale Brodnax, and Mattie Todd who shared their wisdom with me and the young ladies who posed these questions. Thank you to Milledge Dixon for editing this work.

Blessings to you all.

THE GENERATIONS MEET
Life Lessons from our Mothers Gardens

An old adage says, "A fool learns from his own mistakes, but a wise man learns from the mistakes of others." In a quest to breed wise, strong and educated teenagers, this statement can be expanded to include not only the lessons learned from mistakes, but also the lessons learned from successes, challenges, history and experience. The expansion of this thought was the premise upon which I was working when I conceived the idea of *The Generations Meet*. While working with troubled girls, I discovered that most were from homes where parental support was negligible. Some were urban dwellers; others lived in economic excess, and most lived somewhere in between. Regardless of their address, they were besieged by the same problems: peer pressure, drugs, sex, parental neglect, teenage pregnancy, abuse and a myriad of other concerns.

Through various conversations, observations, counseling situations and research, I began to realize that most of the girls were struggling with their transition into womanhood. Most had questions that could be classified in three subject areas: life, love and longevity. The standard for these girls was to take their questions to their peers, who often did not have any more experience in these areas than they did. I began to analyze my struggles with the same questions and poll my friends and colleagues about their experiences. Soon, a pattern emerged. I discovered that, in past generations, girls were guided into womanhood by mothers, grandmothers, neighbors, elderly aunts and teachers. However, wisdom-yielding women—whom my generation too often took for granted—were virtually absent from the lives of these girls. This project was designed to provide the missing inter-generational wisdom to help young women and girls go on improving. While it is easy to point the finger at parents, ineffective churches, bad schools and popular culture. The reality is we are experiencing a tragedy and blame is never as worthwhile as remedy.

I wanted the girls with whom I was working to have the benefit of the "mother-wit" that guided and sheltered others, as well as myself, through the transitional teenage years. My goal was to present an array of differing perspectives, so each girl might take emotional refuge in an enriching life lesson, which she could choose to make her own. As one who firmly believes that "people who know better do better," I know that in such added awareness lies the ability to stabilize the cornerstones that girls place in their lives as they step into womanhood. The women interviewed were willing to provide the knowledge and wisdom; the girls could then supply their own meaning. Even if the girls disagreed with everything that was said, they would do so while thinking about "the issues" and becoming clearer about their views, boundaries, goals and life circumstances.

In order to start the dialogue and address their concerns, I organized a small group of girls and asked them to develop a list of questions that they would ask if they had a chance to talk to some of the wisest women in the world. I then identified the wise women in our midst. They are women living life undaunted by trials and tribulations. They are women who have continued to emerge triumphantly through changing times (before automobiles, television and computers). I wanted them to tell their stories of courage and survival, and about the insights and lessons they learned along the way.

The wisdom these women possess is virtually an untapped abundance of knowledge. I recall how my mother once brought this reality to my attention, asking, "Baby, if I have been downtown one hundred times, and you've never been, why wouldn't you let me show you its short-cuts, landmarks and potholes?" I wanted to help these girls recognize both the adverse potholes and the worthwhile landmarks along life's journey.

After the questions were compiled, I found wise and knowledgeable women of varying backgrounds and cultures (MD's, Ph.D.'s, housewives, battered women, artists, government workers, cancer survivors, women in prison, recovering addicts, etc.) "Grey Counselors" is the name I coined for these wonderful women. They answered questions about love, sex, joy, sorrow and everything in between. They graciously shared their wisdom and some of their most intimate secrets. The wisdom of the ages is embedded in their stories. In many instances, we are learning the lessons from the women who have paved the way to many of the freedoms modern women enjoy.

The questions included:

1 . How can I build a better relationship with my mother?

2 . How can I show my mother that I'm responsible, so I can get out of the house more?

3 . What can you tell me about statutory rape?

4 . What age did you fall in love and how did you know it was love that you felt?

5 . Do you feel that you got a chance to achieve all of your life goals?

6 . Why do you think teenagers don't listen to their parents?

7 . How has getting older changed your viewpoints?

8 . At what age would you advise a girl to get married?

9 . Should I tell my parents that I'm not a virgin and that I'm currently sexually active?

1 0 . What do you regret most as you look over your life?

1 1 . What is your life's greatest joy and sorrow?

1 2 . Is it important for a woman to have a husband or boyfriend in her life?

1 3 . What is the best advice anyone ever gave you?

1 4 . What is the best way to raise children?

1 5 . If you won a lottery, which entitled you to 10 minutes with congress and other political leaders, what would you say to them?

1 6 . What do you wish young women understood about life, love and longevity?

Each woman engaged the subjects according to her beliefs. These interviews are enlightening, encouraging, affirming and educational. They will appeal to women in all stages of their lives: young girls trying to find their way, middle-aged women, young women with children, empty nesters and women on the verge of retirement. Additionally, this book could serve as a discussion guide for mothers and daughters or teachers and students. They could discuss the interviews and the questions and develop a deeper understanding of how and why the generations can and need to meet. There are, to my knowledge, no books on the market that take an intergenerational approach, where teenagers and the elderly are targeted for dialogue from which others not in either group can read, learn and benefit.

When I started this project, I wanted it to provide assistance and knowledge to the girls in my counseling groups. But as I began to work with the project and interviewed more women, I became empowered by their stories and their wisdom.

I believe that a tremendous wealth of information and wisdom is locked up in nursing homes and other places where we hide our elderly. In other countries, age is revered, but in America, youth and the look of youth are what are held in high esteem. With *The Generations Meet*, the wisdom of the ages can be released upon a hungry and waiting public.

With all your science can you tell me how it is, and whence it is,

that light comes into the soul?

--Franz Fanon

Myrna Bentley
I Am Woman

I can rub and scrub this house 'til it's shining like a dime,

Feed the baby, grease the car and powder my face at the same time

Get all dressed up, go out and swing 'til 4:00 am and, then,

Lay down at five, jump up at six and start all over again

'Cause I'm a woman!

W-O-M-A-N, I'll say it again.

These words, from Peggy Lee's blues hit "I'm A Woman," immediately come to mind whenever I think of Myrna. I met her in a study group. We met once a week to study different books, thought forms and spiritual paths. The group was an interesting and eclectic cross section of women and men, who believe our lives are influenced by our thoughts and where we choose to focus our emotional energies. This group was always one of the high points of my week. I admired many of the members of the group, especially Myrna. Her strong feminine presence was attractive. She is not a damsel in distress or a 'girly girl,' but a strong woman who knows what she wants. She is not dependent or needy, yet she appreciates the company of a strong man. Myrna is always immaculately dressed: perfect hair and make-up, an ageless beauty and, unlike those with the tight multi-face-lifted look, she is a classy natural beauty.

I had known Myrna about a year when someone mentioned that she was seventy years old. I did not believe it; I was convinced that Myrna had to be in her forties. Then one night in class, Myrna made an off-handed comment about looking "good for her age." I was shocked when I realized that she was not in my age group. There had to be some well-guarded secret: maybe she'd found the "fountain of youth." Therefore, when this project came about, Myrna was at the top of my list of potential interviewees. From my experiences with her, I knew her to be shockingly honest and open, and I knew a lot could be gleaned from a conversation with her.

Myrna is very active. She works out with a strength trainer, does yoga for flexibility, and paints to develop her creative side. Laughter is extremely important to her and she loves a good dirty joke. She gives demonstrations and classes on handwriting analysis. She has two grandchildren, an attractive and adoring boyfriend and a beautiful home in an upscale Atlanta suburb.

When I arrived for the interview, Myrna was wearing a stylish gray pants suit with matching high heeled strappy sandals. The sweater jacket was swung over her shoulder and the white turtleneck was tied at her left side, making a design that looked like a rose. As usual, her hair was perfectly coiffed, and her make-up was flawless. We sat down to talk in her lovely home, scented with rich candles and the smells of Christmas.

Myrna says, in her interview, that she believes that she will be the best looking eighty-year-old around. I'm sure that scientists and naysayers will say that what she thinks has no bearing on her body or her looks. They would probably say it has more to do with her genes, her diet and exercise patterns. However, Myrna believes the way she thinks is the big secret to her youthfulness. I can't prove either perspective, nor shall I try to, but I do know that what one believes affects how one feels. I can say that Myrna, at seventy-two, is well on her way to being the best looking eighty-year-old I've ever seen.

Myrna Bentley

Myrna Bentley

Myrna. . .

Janice: To start the interview process I want you to tell me anything that you would want someone to know if they were writing your life story: your background, family of origin, the time in which you were born, a brief overview of your life.

I belong to a very small percentage of people that were born into a loving family: my brother, my mom, my dad and me. We were so normal, no dysfunction to speak of, though I was very shy as a little girl. I really hated going anywhere if I did not know the people, like a birthday party where there were strange children. I would freeze and feel like dying until my mother would finally come to get me. Somewhere around age twenty-five, the pendulum did swing the other way, and I became very outgoing. You've heard of silence-breakers. When nobody is saying anything and the room is strained and quiet, I was always the one trying to make them laugh. I also wanted to have the cutest outfit, to tell the funniest jokes, to be the biggest flirt. I really tried to be the life of the party. Thank goodness, somewhere along the way my pendulum sort of settled down. Maybe it's called growing up. I do like to think that I still have a good sense of humor and can see the fun in things.

Janice: How long where you married?

Almost 30 years. My husband died at forty-nine. So I've been a widow for twenty-three, twenty-four years. I live by myself. In a way, I feel like I have always lived by myself. My husband was always gone, and the running of the house and the raising of the boys was pretty much up to me. One time, I called my husband to say the front yard was flooding and the sewer was backing up in the bathroom. He said, "What do you want me to do? You've got the yellow pages just like I do." So, I learned how to take care of the house and the children. Unfortunately, they don't feel like they had much of a father. He was always there if they got put in jail or landed in the hospital, but that was about it. If you ask me why I'm doing so good for my age, I would say that it really comes down to the way you think, totally to the way you think.

Janice: And what age are you?

Seventy-two in January 2003. One thing that helped me get through those first big birthdays was this: My daddy used to say that a woman did not reach her prime until she was thirty-five. This got me through the thirtieth birthday, and I figured that after you reached your prime, you had at least ten years to enjoy it. That got me through my fortieth. After that, birthdays really didn't make much difference.

Speaking of my Dad, he was such a cut-up. My mom was straight-laced and Mid-Victorian. I remember when she made my first strapless evening dress, she nearly cried. She thought she was sending me straight to the hell. On the other hand, my dad and I used to love to tell dirty jokes. We would get off in the corner and tell these jokes and we'd just laugh and laugh, while my mother and my brother, who was born an old man, would roll their eyes and look at us like we were really not to be dealt with. I still love a good dirty joke. I worked for thirteen years at the Guest Quarters Hotel, which is no longer in Atlanta. It was Atlanta's first all-suite hotel. If somebody in the office would tell a good joke, I would travel straight through the office telling everybody. I miss that. Unfortunately, I seldom hear a good joke anymore. But, I used to love them.

Because of my early shyness, I was very insecure. The only thing that made me feel good about myself was my clothes. My mom used to sew like an angel. We were not a wealthy family. We were okay, but we had to watch the budget and she would make me clothes that the rich girls envied. So a lot of my security was in my clothes. I still have to admit that I don't like to go anywhere if I don't have something new to wear. Give me something new and I'm a lot happier.

Getting back to the subject of how you think. I just recently listened to some teaching tapes on life and what the world's all about - that I have found so very, very exciting. They're from the Hicks family in Texas, and when I look back, I think that I have always practiced some of this without realizing what I was doing. The teaching is not new. It's all in the Bible. Do onto others and you can be damn well sure it will be done onto you. I changed it just a little bit. It's, 'bread cast onto the waters comes back, threefold,' 'ask and you will receive.' Of course, you have to be in a happy vibration or it will just stop at your front door.

The first positive-thinking book I ever read was Maxwell Maltz's *Psycho-Cybernetics*. He compared the mind to a computer. He said, "If you don't feed it in, you won't get it back. If you don't program it, you won't stand much chance of getting it back." So that started me trying to think positive. It really is important what you let yourself focus on. It may sound naïve or even a bit stupid, but one time many years ago, my husband was in the hospital for three weeks. He was in great pain and they ended up doing an appendectomy on him, only to find that he had ileitis. They had to pull his intestines out just like a hose because he was fat. (Did you know that a man grows his fat around his inner organs whereas a woman has a muscular lining over her organs that keep the fat on the outside?) He was so sick, but they found out what was wrong with him. It was not his appendix. He had ileitis, which is inflamed intestines. The doctor said the operation was the worst thing they could have done and that they could have lost him at any time. I was so sure that he would get well; it never entered my mind that I might lose him. The point to this story is that I have been pretty much a non-worrier all of my life.

Take the subject of money. I will have to admit that my mom helped me a lot. When we had financial problems, she would pull up in my driveway and ask me if I had plenty of money. I would say, "Yeah, I think so." You know I didn't want to say yes. She would pull out a twenty dollar bill, which was a lot of money back then. And she would say, "Here, I can't stand for you to be without money." So, because of her, I never felt poor. I never had to worry, worry, and worry, about money. Wayne Dyer has said that if you think poor, you'll never be rich. So I guess my mom sort of kept me from thinking poor. I knew that if anything ever went wrong, she was always going to be there for me. Dyer also said that if you think fat you'll never be thin. I always thought I had a pretty cute figure. It's not quite as cute now as I would like it to be, but I'm working on it. I still have a closet full of size eights I'm trying to get into. Unfortunately, I've gone to the tens. The weight gain did not start until I went through a period of not thinking very positive about myself. When my daddy died, who had been looking after my invalid mother for years, all of a sudden, looking after her was now on my shoulders. I had two and a half years of being caretaker for my mother. I didn't have to move in with her because we lived close, but from four o'clock 'til nine o'clock every day, I went to her house to take care of all things. I cooked dinner, left food for her for the next day, washed, ironed, cleaned, paid bills etc., etc. As I look back, I'm not sorry. I would feel guilty had I not taken care of her because she had always been so very good to me.

I do live alone, and have since my husband died and my boys left home. I have been dating a man for about twenty-three years and people ask, "Why don't you get married?" There are a lot of reasons. He's a perfectionist. He's sort of a neat freak. For example, he washes his tools before he puts them up and he never finishes a job without putting everything away. Me, I'll leave my tools in the carport and they might stay there for three weeks, and, though I hate to admit it, they probably will not be washed when they do get put away. And last, but not least, because of my husband's business, I was pretty much always left alone when I was married—except for the two boys, of course. So, I have been used to having a lot of space to myself for all of my grown-up years.

Janice: How old are your sons?

One's forty-five and one's forty-two. I was talking to Reid today and I told him that you were going to interview me because of my age. Tacky, Tacky, Tacky.

Janice: It's not because of your age, because there are plenty of women that are your age. It's your vivaciousness.

Well, shoot, I appreciate that. He said, "Don't you think you're doing as good as you're doing because you were sixty-five when you had your first grandchild?" And I thought, maybe. I do know that I never knew I could fall in love so fast as when I first saw those babies. I was blessed with a little boy from one son, then a little girl two weeks later from the other son – one of each. I didn't think that I would have any grandchildren because both my boys waited so long. I'm probably a little closer to the little boy because I was number one on the babysitting list in that family, whereas as I was number two (her mother was number one) in the other family. That makes a big difference. These children are my heart. I absolutely adore them. One of my favorite sayings is, "It's hard not to adore somebody that adores you." We've got that going, the little guy and me. He's almost seven now. I can't believe he's that big.

You asked me what things have I done. A couple of things come to mind, though there is nothing worth bragging about. When I was thirty-five, my mom gave me two books because I had expressed an interest in both of them. It was Mother's Day and she picked up the two books and each child gave me a book. One was on yoga and the other was on handwriting analysis. Believe it or not, I still do both. I didn't read the book on handwriting for a long time because I became interested in the yoga first and loved it. If I could do it over again, I would take Yoga for my whole life. When I was about twenty-five, I took a class in it and it lasted about seven or eight weeks. I did not sign up again, and I wasn't disciplined enough to do it at home. Back then, I was like a rubber band. I could do all the positions, no problem. Now, I do it twice a week and hope to never quit doing it. It keeps me flexible. I was getting to the point where it was necessary to pull myself up and out to get out of the car. I could tell Chuck was noticing; that was making me look on the old side. I didn't like it, either. Besides the physical benefits, the Yoga also gives me the quiet time to meditate and go inward.

I take a yoga class twice a week. A friend of mine teaches it. I do think that we have a good vibration going. It makes a difference when you get one. I really, really, really, really believe in vibrations. Where you choose to vibrate determines what you get and what you can expect from life. I believe that this includes health, relationships, money, and all the things you wish for from life. This is hard to accept if your life is not going very well, but I believe that you can look at somebody and their life, and tell what kind of vibrations they've been working on. The secret is to keep your thoughts and feelings focused on the happier things in your life. Appreciate anything and everything that you can. I've been really trying to do this and am doing pretty well. I'm healthy; I do take a lot of supplements to stay that way, but I sometimes wonder if I really need them. However, I've been taking them for so many years, now I'm afraid to stop. My son says, "Mom, what do you need with all this stuff?" He rolls his eyes when I come home with something new.

Then, he said something that might be really, really true. He said, "If you believe it's gonna make you well, it probably will." Here we go, back to that old saying," As a man thinketh, so is he."

Now, ask me your questions.

Janice: O.K. These questions are the questions from some girls I work with. They are all between the ages of 12 and 18. Firstly, do you feel as if you got a chance to finish all of your life goals?

I was never what you would call real "goal oriented." Women did not have careers when I was young. I actually majored in home economics in college. To be a good wife and mother was all I thought I was supposed to do. I can say that the things that I really wanted to do, I now can do pretty well.   I am really good about looking at someone's handwriting and getting the facts straight about them. I can easily entertain a party. I'm a good handwriting analyst, if I do say so myself, and it was something that I really wanted to do. It cost $500 to take the course. Studying it made me able to understand people and their fears and defenses, which has been such a plus in my life. Better than that, though, it gave me insight into myself which was more valuable than many, many 500 dollars. I learned how my fears were paralyzing me. Fear of criticism was the worst. I just lived in total fear of what other people thought, and you could see it in my handwriting, how big it was. It was a fear trait that made me sarcastic. Sarcasm is often the #1 defense against this fear, and I had it. Since understanding this about myself, I find it hard, even if giving a lecture, to give a good example of sarcasm. It's totally gone. I still can get it, that fear of disapproval, but now, I spot it the minute it starts. I say to myself, "Uh-oh, here we go." Then I make myself think of something else. *Don't go there. Those people are not worried about you. They are not thinking about what you said or did. They're off living their life.* I can give you one good lecture on that, on how to be yourself and how to deal with some of these fear traits and understand the defenses that we build up.

When I think of the problems that are out there now, the anthrax, the bombing, the buildings coming down, I think, *do I worry or don't worry.* I don't worry. I always felt that when my time comes, then I'll go. That'll be it. My biggest statement is that I don't mind dying; I just don't want to be sick. My daddy, he did it. He did it one way and my mom did it another. My mom was housebound for fourteen years. My dad dropped dead at 86. He meditated, went to bed and, boom, dropped dead.

Back to the subject of goals, age has nothing to do with it. There is opportunity to go for things you want every day of your life. I do wish maybe that I had had more belief in my ability to get anything I wanted if I had wanted it bad enough. Now, my main goal is to stay connected to my higher self or my source energy. That is when the little and the big things you ask for seem to fall into your lap.

Janice: What do you think is one of the biggest mistakes young women make in love?

Thinking that going all the way means the same thing to a man that it means to a woman. Especially young girls. They think that when they fall into bed, that that is it. They think they have given him this wonderful gift and they think he will stay with them for life. It is just a notch in the kid's belt. He is not affected that way. I've been in every corner that you can be with a man. I've been the wife that has been cheated on, I've been the mistress, I've been the neglected, the devoted, whatever. *A man is only loyal and monogamous for one reason, because he wants to be.* If he adores you, he'll be loyal.

Janice: What advice would you give teenagers on relationships?

We need to work on teaching our children that the way they feel can be the most important and reliable guidance system that they will ever have. You do have to find your happiness from within yourself. If you think someone else is going to make you happy, you are in for a rude awakening. The only person that you can control is yourself. If you can ever learn to refuse to let another person be the reason for your happiness or your unhappiness, you will have achieved something very wonderful.

Anything that happens to you, anything, from the day you are born till the day you die, is what you have attracted to yourself. What you are supposed to do is learn and grow from it. I believe that you pick your family. You pick your environment. In your soul's knowledge, before you came in, you said," Ah, I'll go over there." I'll really grow in that environment. It's hard to believe, but it keeps you from feeling victimized. If you married a man that beat the hell out of you, you still have to say "I did it to myself." You had to say, "Yes," when he asked you to marry him... If you work for a company and they don't respect you, they don't promote you. They do this that you don't like and they don't do that and you feel all of this resentment building up, remember, you don't have to stay. You can walk away any time you want to. If you stay, realize that there must be reasons that you are staying. Look for the good. I like the paycheck, I like my friends, I like the hours, the location. Accept the responsibility for where you find yourself, and then you will never blame anybody else.

Don't let yourself build up resentment because resentment will only hurt you. It doesn't hurt anybody else. It is feeling sorry for yourself, playing the role of victim. The worst thing about the trait of resentment is that it is like a fungus. It may start over one particular thing, but if allowed, it will fester and grow until you find yourself bitter, angry and not trusting anybody. I often thought that because I do handwriting so well that I should volunteer up at the Link, which is a teenaged house that works with children, teenagers. Anyway, you can get a lot of insight into yourself through looking at yourself through your handwriting. You can see depression, you can see anger, and you can see resentment.

Janice: Why do you think that teenagers don't listen to their parents?

This is not something new. It's been going on for generations and generations. Why don't they listen to their parents? Because their parents try to control them. The parents want the children to behave by their rules in order for them to be happy. The children don't want that responsibility. It truly does go in one ear and out the other. The best way to teach your children is by example. Instead of screaming and bitching at the kids about what they are not doing or what they are doing, they need to praise, appreciate and love. Pick out the things about the child that they can praise, and use the positive to teach. Parents should also pick out the things they can be happy over in their own lives. If they are happy, loving, appreciative people, I just think it rubs off on the children. I do watch a lot of TV. Sometimes I watch a show just because the TV is on. Some of these talk shows get these troubled children on. They are the most defiant. They are sleeping around. They're using drugs. They're often as young as thirteen years old, and they're just awful. But, if you listen to some of the mothers that bring them there, you'll understand. They talk nasty, they're angry and they're worse than the children. They're not good examples. The children that are being born today are coming in with a faster vibration, and will do just fine if we can take a more understanding approach about what they are capable of.

Janice: What makes these children vibrate higher?

They can handle more than we think they can. They can handle the rap music and the violent movies and things that we think are ruining them. *It's only that when a child goes wrong we have to find something or somebody to blame.* Just remember, there are more good children than there are bad ones, and all the bad ones can become good ones when they find their way.

Janice: How has getting older changed your viewpoint?

Well, I realize a lot of things don't matter. There was a day when I wouldn't go out of the house without having the right clothes on. Now I will go to Yoga class in exercise clothes and then do errands on the way home. You know, nobody said a thing to me about how I looked. I still have a way to go, but I do know that there are so many things that really don't matter. I realize my children don't need me. When I get on an airplane I say to the kids, "Spend my money wisely if anything happens. Have a good time. Do not worry. Do not grieve. I don't fear death." I don't know if when the day comes, I'll say, 'Oh no, I don't want to go.' But, right now I think it'll be okay. My responsibilities are gone. The responsibilities in my life are over. My children are raised. Sure, I'd like to see my grandchildren graduate and marry, even be great-grandmother, but I was late getting started on that. Besides, If only they had given me babies ten years earlier, there was much more I could have done for them. I would have been out walking, riding bicycles, doing things with them. Now, I don't do that. You should have seen me trying to play hop scotch the other day. Trying to go down and grab a rock with one foot in the air.

Janice: If you had to do all over again, what changes would you make?

I never thought about that. I married a man and he didn't know how to love me or the children because he didn't love himself. He died young because he thought he'd be a millionaire by the time he was forty, and was not. He owned a restaurant. He was gone 'til 3:00 am every night, and then he slept 'til 10:00 am. Then, he was gone again. I was young and naïve enough to think it that was all right. But I realize I wouldn't have grown as much if I had a man who came home at five or six o'clock every night. I would have been so dependent on him and in a little house-wifey rut. But this way, I became creative. I did artistic things. I wasn't an artist, but I did things like make posters for the children. I decorated the Garden Club Scrapbook, made Christmas decorations, things like that. In fact, my husband would say, "Can't you do something that you could make money at?" I was always doing something: making decorations for the Christmas dance, Christmas presents, something like that. What would I do differently? I wouldn't have grown if I hadn't married a man who neglected me. I wouldn't have studied the handwriting analysis. I wouldn't have done a lot of those things. So I can't say I wouldn't have married him. I think it might have been good that I married a man who neglected me. I would take yoga when I was growing up. I would do exercises with Jack LuLanne - he was the first one on television that did exercises. Now everybody is into exercising: muscles in the arms and bodybuilding and abs and stuff like that. That wasn't there when I was young. But, if I had it to do over again, I'd always do something to feel vital. That's what I'd do all over again. I think studying the handwriting was the best thing I ever did.

Janice: At what age did you fall in love, and how did you know it was love?

I fell in love when I was a junior in high school and married that man when I was nineteen. Honestly, I think that I didn't think anybody else would ever ask. And, also, he got me to have sex with him before we were married, and that was an absolute no-no. And I felt like I had to marry him to make it okay, to make it legitimate. My children don't know that. Not that they would care.

Janice: How did you know it was love?

I don't think I did. He did. He made up his mind that he was going to marry me. We broke up once, and he went over and told my mother, this was pretty unusual for a senior in high school. He went over and talked to my mother. He told her that he was going to marry me. I was sort of just sucked in. My mother cried when I showed her my ring. He was not her pick for me. But if I hadn't married him, I might not be the person that I am. You attract what you're supposed to have. You get what your vibration asks for. My vibration was not where it was supposed to be. I was shy, shy and insecure. I was a little church mouse. I was disappointed; my husband was a drinker, a beer drinker. I would count his beers and pout, pout, pout. I would give him these looks when we were out with a group. He finally laid it on the line one night when we were on our way home. He said, "If you're unhappy, you damn better well keep it to yourself. I will not have you airing our dirty laundry out in public." Man, he came on so strong, I stopped doing that. I was scared and you don't need to be that way.

Janice: At what age should a girl get married?

Right now, the longer you wait, the better you do. Back then, you got married at eighteen or nineteen. The generation before was even earlier. Each case is individual. I wasn't ready. I should have waited. In other words, she should wait until she knows her own mind.

Janice: This young lady wants to know, "how do I open up and share my feelings with my mother?"

Just tell her what you need. For instance, if you tell her you want her to take you in her arms and hold you, she might not give it to you, but at least she knows what's on your mind and where you're coming from.

Janice: Next Question, should I open up to my parents and tell them that I am not a virgin and that I'm currently sexually active?

You know your parents better than I do. Some parents can take it, some can't. Whether you tell her or not, make sure you're taking care of yourself and taking proper precautions. Make sure that you know what you're doing. Know that sex is not love; try to be safe and save some of the things for the man you're going to marry.

Janice: How do you cope with the loss of a love or a lover?

Grieving is always about 'you don't think you know what you're going to do without the person.' In other words, when my husband went into the hospital – not the first time, but another time when he had a heart attack. This time, I knew he might die, and I looked around the waiting room at the different people. Most of them were distraught because they didn't know what they were going to do without the person. It wasn't that they were worried about the person going; they were worried about what they were going to do without the person. It's always a self thing involved with grieving. So, take a look inside yourself and find out what your needs are. And if it's a boyfriend that you lose, know within your heart that someone better is going to come alone. If it was meant to be, then he'd still be there. And if it's a father being taken away, get spiritual, go into meditation, and start meditating. Get quiet and go within your spirit or your heart and ask a question; you'll get an answer. You might not get a voice, but you'll know. If you were close, you'll be close to the spirit, if you weren't close, then look for someone else that you can talk too.

Janice: How do you eliminate stress in your life?

I just do what I want to do. My favorite saying is, "If there is nothing to do, I do nothing." I read, I paint, I watch some of the talk shows. I love Oprah. Oprah has some good topics. I just don't worry.

Janice: How can you instill in young girls to love themselves so they don't look for someone else to do it for them?

Pick one thing that you like about yourself. It can be anything that you like, and focus on that. Then, pick another thing and continue to concentrate on all the good things about yourself.

Janice: How do you maintain a monogamous relationship?

I've already answered that one; a man will only be faithful for one reason, because he wants to. You have to have something going for yourself and the relationship where you decide that, whatever happens, the two of you will work through it—that you're going to stay together. But, that takes two. *Nothing will make a man stray faster than you suspecting him of infidelity. If you are always accusing him of doing something, always worried about him, give him two years and he will do exactly what you accuse him of doing.* I read this in a book so many years ago. So, you see him loyal, you see him as just as faithful and totally devoted to you as you are to him, and chances are a lot better that that's what he will be.

Janice: How do parents instill in their children the morals and values that elderly people where raised with?

Like, how do my children instill in their children the morals I was raised with? Well, morals change. I don't think they should try to do what I was raised with or what my mother was raised with. I don't think they should try to do what I was taught, because I think it was a different time and times have changed too much and we can't go backwards. I think, whatever you teach them, you teach them by example. I think if you are a person with integrity and good traits, it will rub off on the kids.

Janice: What should you do, when you your mother does not act like, nor does she want to be, a mother, and she doesn't protect you?

That's so sad. What do you say to someone like that? What do you say? Does she have someone else that she could talk to? Of course, I would say go to the spiritual side of this. Go to sleep at night and visualize the help that you need, the protection that you need, the love that you need, hopefully coming from your mom, but if not, a mentor. In other words, put the wish out there to God, to the universe, to your higher self, or anything you want to call it, and say "I need help." Say, "I want this, I need this, I would love to have this," and visualize it, see it. Want it and say, "I really would like to have this, could you send me some help? I'd like it to come from my mom, but, if not, family or somebody that could do these things for me. If not, please give me the strength to grow and be strong and be a wonderful person without help." I know that can be hard.

Let me tell you something. I had this little girl, she lived next door. She was the age of my child, and she would come over here and talk to me because I wouldn't judge her like her mom would. She would come over and tell me things about what she was doing that, maybe, her mom wouldn't want her to be doing, and sometimes, she'd just come over to talk. Maybe I was the person she could tell because I wouldn't tell her what to do, I don't know. She came over and told me about a group that she wanted to be a part of in school, but they didn't want any part of her. This was a pretty girl; she was very smart, very quiet. She wanted to be in this clique, and I didn't know what to tell her, except I had read Psycho-Cybernetics, which says 'program it, see it, visualize it, program it and know that it's going to come.' So I told her every night, before you go to sleep, see yourself right in the middle of that group: see them liking you, laughing, having a good time. See it exactly as you would like it to happen. That's all I told her and, after awhile, she came running over to tell me, "Ms. Bentley, it really works!" She said, "They asked me to join the club." I was so proud. It does really work. Just know that, whatever she's going through, she will get beyond it. She'll grow beyond it, love beyond it, and it will be all right. Try to find something to be happy about.

Janice: Okay what do you consider to be the best invention of your lifetime?

Uh, probably the computer, though the TV had more impact on me. When I was married—I mean, I didn't get a TV while I was married, we dated without a television—I knew every movie in town because it was fifty cents a movie and we went every night. So, probably the computer now.

Janice: Your greatest joy?

My little grandson, right now.

Janice: Is it important for a woman to have a husband or boyfriend in her life?

It's nice to have somebody that's interested in you, who needs you a bit and that likes what you've got to offer. But I totally believe that to be happy, you have to be happy by yourself. And, then, if you're lucky you can share it with somebody else.

Janice: What one thing do you wish women understood about life?

Women understood? Or anybody understands?

Janice: Specifically women.

Man, these questions are something else. That we are vibrational beings. And whatever vibration we're at is what we're going to get. So if you want a wonderful life with beautiful relationships and creative success, you have to get yourself in a high vibration that will nail that stuff out.

Janice: What is the one thing you wish women understood about love?

There you go again, Ms. America. These are deep!! Love is caring. . . Don't put demands on people, you look for the good in them, you appreciate them and hope that they appreciate you, good and bad.

Janice: What is your secret to longevity?

Believing. Believing. I believe that I will the best looking eighty-year-old you've ever seen, other than movie stars. I mean, I really think I am going to lick the age barrier.

I started to tell you earlier and forgot about it. My daddy, my cut-up daddy, used to say over and over and over again, a woman doesn't reach her prime until she's thirty-five. So that got me through my thirtieth birthday real easy. And, I figured after you reach your prime you've got at least ten years. So that got me through my fortieth birthday without giving it a second thought; I was in my prime. I mean, I believed it and it happened. I was tough at thirty-eight, thirty-nine, forty, and forty-four. But then, at 50...well, I got through thirty, forty and fifties okay. I was still doing pretty good at fifty. Sixty, I'd learned how by then. At seventy, I thought, "Wow, people are going to think that's old." I really did. I think it was harder for me than any that I've had. "Seventy years old - man you are getting old!" But it really didn't bother me. It really doesn't. Age is a state of mind. If you think you are doing good, you are going to do good. And if you are feeling old and thinking you can't do things, you probably won't.

Janice: I believe it. Okay, what is your recipe for fulfilling life?

You are terrible! Recipe for a fulfilling life? Dare to dream and believe it's going to come true. I didn't know this as a youngster, or I might have dreamt a little more than I did.

Janice: What is the best advice anyone has ever given you?

Well, the positive thinking. The positive thinking, which started when I read *Psycho-Cybernetics* and now I'm into the Abraham Hicks works, which do not focus on anything negative. No criticizing. If somebody has made you mad, you try to go and think of something besides the anger you feel. If you're depressed, you try to look for something that makes you feel better. In other words, you really work at where your mind is and feelings are. And, I wish I had known this when I was a young person, and, yet, I think, in my naïveté, I did a lot of it without knowing what I was doing.

Janice: Is that the one thing you wish you knew, then, that you know now?

Oh, absolutely, yes. Do not let yourself think about anything bad. Do not, do not. And one of the last lessons I was listening to, I listen to these things on tape, said, "But isn't that, sticking your head in the sand?" The answer was, "Call it what you want to, sticking your head in the sand, denial, not facing reality, idiocy, call it anything you want to. But, to keep yourself on a good vibration, you have got to think about something nice. You've got to try to go to a happier place." And it works. This can go for illness, too. If you've got a pain and you focus on that pain, it's going to get worse. You got a pain and you start thinking about it, you say *"Oops, let me think about something else; let me take this pill and think about something else."* And, if you work at it, you can train yourself. It's a full-time job.

Janice: How do you motivate yourself?

If there is something to do, I get motivated. If there is not something to do, I don't. I love my house, I really do. I love decorating it, I love adding something new to it, I love my yard, I love to draw, now, since I just started doing that. There are a lot of things I love to do. I love my Chuck. I haven't said much about him, but, yeah, he's a very big part of my life. And, he is so good to me; I couldn't live in this old house without him because he just takes care of so much of the problems that come about. Even the car. He's such an automobile man, and he'll tell me, "Well, you need new struts," or "You need to have your tires rotated, it's time for this it's time for that." I mean, he's very very helpful to me.

My kids say "Mama would you really like him as much if he wasn't a stud?" (laughter) And I'll never know whether I would or not, maybe not. I've always been a visionary. How things look mean a lot to me. How I look, how they look, how the house looks, how the yard looks. I wish it didn't matter so much, but I think it's a type of person. Maybe it's the right brain, I don't know.

But I really want things pretty. I mean, I can walk through a park, through a building, a landscaping, it doesn't matter, and I just think, *oh that's so pretty*. I'm sure it's not the same with everybody.

Janice: Now this is definitely a Miss America question. What advice do you wish you could give to our political leaders?

Keep your vibration high! And they don't know how to. They are focusing on war and revenge and anger. Oh, yes, it was a terrible thing that happened, and we will never be the same again. But I think fear is the worst thing that could happen to us. I think we have got to concentrate on things other than fear. And look at the good that's come from this tragedy, the way people have bonded together, the way they are kinder, the way they are more supportive and everything to each other. That's good. And maybe, if we send enough thoughts and pray hard enough, the politicians will get insight and wisdom and a gentleness that might help the world.

Janice: What do you think about popular culture: Music, dress the MTV generation, movie stars?

Like Britney Spears and her bare belly and things like that? Every kid wants to look like that and they don't, and that's the pitiful part. If I'd been her age and looked like that, I probably would have done the same damn thing. As far as the piercings, I don't really get that. But ten years from now, when the holes have gone back together, will it really matter?

A long time ago when I was raising my kids somebody said to me, "Ask yourself why you're fighting over hair. . ." See, we used to go through [it] when the kids wanted to wear long hair, when the boys wanted to let their hair grow. Oh, straight parents thought that was terrible and there were many family fights over it. And somebody said, "Ask yourself: ten years from now is it going to matter? Is it going to affect his character whether he had long hair or not?"

And I sort of used that as much as I could. Ten years from now, is it going to matter that they listen to rap, is it really making them bad? I don't think that's the cause, although that's what gets blamed for it. I think the home is probably the most important; in fact, I had a spiritual teacher tell me at one time that there are three churches in everybody's mind. The first one is in your heart, the second one is in your home, and the third one is where you go on Sunday. If you can take care of the first two, the third one will be okay or not okay. It won't matter if you've got your heart and your home in good shape.

Janice: Tell me a little bit about what your daily routine is like?

Well, three days a week, I have things that I have to get up and get ready to do. I go to Yoga twice a week and I got Art class in Cummings, which is 30 miles away, on Mondays. So, those are my days when I really get up and have to have the hair washed and the makeup on and be ready to roll by nine o'clock.

So, I usually get up at seven and do the things that I do. You know the saying, "You can tell how old a woman is by how long it takes her to get ready." There is a lot of truth in that. And those three days, I don't usually get back here and ready to roll until between 1:30 and 3:00 pm. So, those days are pretty busy, and I like that.

And, then, I make phone calls and Chuck, bless his heart, he gets off sort of early. He gets off work sometimes at 3:00, and if he comes early, my day is chopped off. I really love it when he doesn't come till 5:30, you know, when he has something he has to do and he comes at 5:30 and, then, we go out to eat. He doesn't like TV. Sometimes, we go to a meeting at Sam's. Sometimes we go to Stein Mart; he loves Stein Mart. He shops at Stein Mart, and that's our big day, when we go to Stein Mart - eat dinner and go to Stein Mart. He doesn't like TV, but I'm really trying to get him to watch some of the things to make him laugh. That's how I got into baseball, because that was the one thing we'd do together. Now, I'm a big Braves fan. Never thought when I was young I would ever watch a baseball game. Now, I just totally enjoy them. In fact, I think I enjoy them more than he does, now.

But, my days are totally [prioritized] by what needs to be done. I'll be honest, I watch soap operas. And you all don't want to put this in there, that's terrible, but I try to rewrite them when I watch them. I try to think ahead of what they are going to say. I mean, I love the beauty. They are all so pretty and their houses are beautiful and they've all got money. You know, I can enjoy game shows. I love "The Wheel", and some of those things. I love "Regis and Kelly" in the morning. I just think they are so adorable

Janice: So 80 is going to be kickin huh?

On one side or the other. (laughter)

Janice: You were telling me—all the questions are over, but I wanted to get something else on tape that you were telling me earlier. You were telling me about '*If a woman wants to be sexy. . .*'

She has to think sexy. The best example of that—now, see, I do watch TV, and I'll tell people who don't watch TV, "Just use me as a screening process, I'll pull the good off of TV and tell you about it."

But watch Star Jones on BET. She's black, she's big, she's beautiful and she is so sexy. Why is she sexy? Because she thinks she is sexy. Sexiness is a state of mind. But, then, everything is a state of mind. Feeling old is a state of mind. Feeling young is a state of mind. Feeling romantic is state of mind. You know, they say that romantic sex is not in your pants, it's between your ears. It's how you're thinking, how you're feeling, how you're wanting, and so...what was the question?

Janice: Myrna, you look at least 30 years younger than what your chronological age states.

Oh, oh, oh! Don't get that camera on a close-up. But, the thing is, I'm not sending out a message that I want a man. I've got a man, and I'm totally happy with him. And so, I don't send out any messages. You've heard people talking about the vibrations or the chemistry. I've heard men say they can walk in a room full of women and know which one is available. It's all in the way you feel about yourself, it really is. I mean, let's face it; some are blessed more than others. There *are* the Britney Spears in the world, but we all know that everybody is not blessed with a gorgeous face and a magnificent body.

There was a book written many years ago called *The Sensuous Woman*, and she [the author] mentions, in the book, that she is not really pretty. Yet, she mastered the art of sex to the point that every man she ran into thought that she was delightful. She gave you all her tricks, which I really think should be censored from your report.

Lessons from Myrna

You are what you think you are.

I really, really, really, believe in vibrations. Where you choose to vibrate determines what you get and what you can expect from life. I believe that, and this includes health, relationships, money and all the things you wish for from life. . . . The secret is to keep your thoughts and feelings focused on the happier things in your life. Appreciate anything and everything that you can.

Sex never means the same to men as it does to women.

They (young girls) think that when they fall into bed that that is it. They think they have given him this wonderful gift and they think he will stay with them for life. It is just a notch in the kid's belt. He is not affected that way.

A man will soon become what you accuse him of being.

But nothing will make a man stray faster than you suspecting him of infidelity. If you are always accusing him of doing something, always worried about him, give him two years and he will do exactly what you accuse him of doing.

A man is only loyal and monogamous for one reason.

I've been in every corner that you can be with a man. I've been the wife that has been cheated on, I've been the mistress, I've been the neglected, the devoted, the whatever. And I've learned a man is only loyal and monogamous for one reason, because he wants to be.

Age has nothing to do with it.

There is opportunity to go for things you want every day of your life.

We need to teach our children that the way they feel can be the most important and reliable guidance system they will ever have.

You have to find your happiness from within yourself. If you think someone else is going to make you happy you are in for a rude awakening. The only person that can control is you. If you can ever learn to refuse to let another person be the reason for your happiness or your unhappiness, you will have achieved something very wonderful.

FAVORITE BOOKS

Psycho-Cybernetics by Maxwell Maltz

The Sensuous Woman by J

Discussion

1 . **What do you really think about you?**

    A. Does what you think have an affect or an effect on your life?

    B. Does what you think about you, influence what others think about you?

    C. What do your actions say about what you believe about yourself?

    D. Is there a contradiction between what you think about you, how you act and how you treat you?

    E. How can you change your thoughts and your actions?

2 . **Are the views concerning sex for boys different from the views of girls?**

    A. How do girls generally view sex? Boys?

    B. What are some of the motivations for girls having sex?

    C. How do those motivations differ from boys?

D. What should girls know and do before engaging in sex?

E. What is the difference between sex and love?

F. How does having sex affect a girl's reputation? A boy's?

3. **Has anyone ever accused you of anything to which you were not guilty?**

A. How did that make you feel?

B. What did you do?

C. Were you able to convince them of your innocence?

D. What was the final outcome?

4. **What steps can you take to insure your partner is faithful?**

A. Are there ever good reasons to cheat?

B. What should you do if your partner is unfaithful?

C. Have you ever cheated? And if so why?

5. **Pick one thing you really like about yourself?**

A. Concentrate on it and describe how it makes you feel.

B. What would happen if you spent daily time focusing on your good points?

    C. Make a list of the things you like about 3 close friends and your parents?

6 .   **What would you like to achieve this year?**

    A. What are the things you need to do to meet this goal?

    B. What needs to be done first?

    C. Who do you need to contract to assist you?

7 .   **What did you learn from Myrna?**

    A. What did you like about her?

    B. What didn't you like?

    C. Was there anything you didn't understand?

    D. Is there anything you'd ask her for clarification or concerning topic not covered in the interview?

    E. Are there any points that you disagree with her on?

Write a message to Myrna in 100 words or less.

What matters is not to know the world, but to change it.

--Franz Fanon

Louise Strickland
Battered and Bruised, But Not Broken

I had not met Louise before our interview. I mentioned the project to a friend and she immediately, said: "I know a woman that you must interview." When I arrived for the interview, I discovered Louise to be a small-framed woman, suffering from crippling arthritis. Her hands are arthritic and she has extremely limited mobility. However, her physical condition is overshadowed by her presence; it is so warm, inviting and calming that it is almost palatable. I never felt like Louise and I were strangers; I felt like I was settling down to converse with an old friend I hadn't seen in awhile.

Louise was a nurse by profession. While in college, she met a young theology student, and they were married and had six children. Her husband was an ordained minister plagued by mental illness. He was extremely abusive to Louise and their children, yet she remained in this volatile and abusive relationship for over thirty years. Even though Louise was a battered woman, she is not a broken or mousy woman. On the contrary, Louise is a woman with great courage, wisdom and a clear and articulate mode of expression.

Louise's interview was very impressive. It was clear that she harbored no ill will; she had forgiven her husband, sought to minimize the damage in her children and dedicated her life to helping other battered women. She led her family through a study of her favorite book, *Codependent No More*, by Melody Beattie, to help them heal from their familial dysfunction. Louise did not make excuses for the past, but was focused on the "now." In the interview, she opened her life most graciously and shared her struggles, beliefs, children, disease and the kernel of hope she has for the future. Her favorite saying is "This, too, shall pass." Her responses to the questions were poignant and direct, and I loved every minute of her interview. She has a passion for people and a worldview that emphasizes justice, equality and acceptance. I kept thinking, "I would love for her to be my senator or representative." It was women like her that I had in mind when I first conceived this project. I was truly blessed to make her acquaintance.

I marvel at how someone could live through thirty years of physical, emotional and verbal abuse, crippling arthritis, twenty-three joint surgeries, cancer, a double mastectomy, congestive heart failure, a schizophrenic son, a cheating husband and still call life "sweet." Surely abuse, the threat of abuse and the stress associated with abuse may have played an extraordinary role in her physical ailments and limitations. However, there was no bitterness, hatred or blaming. She said she is still concerned about her ex-husband and prays for him. Louise wishes she had left her husband: she wishes she had known she could have made it. Her desire is for no person to endure what she did, but if they should happen to, she prays that they find help and life's sweetness again. Louise's interview made me hopeful; I realized that whatever hand life's cards deal, "this, too, shall pass."

Louise Strickland

Louise. . .

Janice: Tell me about your life. What would anyone writing your life story need to know?

Alright, my life... Well, I had a perfectly wonderful childhood: I was just loved and knew I was loved. We didn't have a lot of money, but we had enough to eat and even went through the Depression without too many problems. I lived out in the country and had to entertain myself a lot because there weren't neighbors with children. I think that taught me a lot about relating, by just turning within myself. I used to cut out paper dolls from the Sears and Roebuck catalog. We had stair steps and I would build a family on each step. The family members had all kinds of experiences that I had heard about on the radio or whatever—that's all we had, was the radio.

I pretended that the families had problems and they had to work through their problems. It was a strange childhood, in a way. I loved going to school because there were people there that I could relate to. I was always in the middle of everything. I had a wonderful growing up time and a happy teenage life. We didn't have any problems with fighting against parents or getting pregnant or anything. I just assumed that I wouldn't get pregnant if I didn't have sex until I got through college. I really was given a great childhood, and I'm glad I had those memories to fall back on.

I went to college and I graduated from Emory University with a B.S. in nursing. The first job I had was as a head nurse at Emory Hospital. The next work I did was teaching nursing, and while I was teaching at Emory, I fell in love with a young theology student. It just looked as if the life ahead was going to be so wonderful. We got married and we had a good two and a half years when things were so wonderful, before we had children. Then, after we had our first child, things weren't so wonderful after all. My husband was often irritated by the child or by some of the work he was doing, because we were assigned to churches where people gave him a lot of trouble. I soon discovered that my husband had a bad temper.

Not many months after our first child was born, I saw that temper and lack of self-control for myself. Our little girl had been crying and wouldn't go to sleep. I had tried to get her to sleep without success and he was trying to get her quiet. Then he became angry and went and held the baby over her crib and just dropped her. That was a telling moment in my life. All of a sudden, I realized I had married a man who had a problem, and I didn't know what to do. We did talk about it; however, at that time, there weren't a lot of marriage or anger-management counselors. He always promised to do better, and through the years he tried. But as time went on, his temper became out-of-control, until it finally destroyed our marriage. In the interim, we had six children, and in between those bad times, we had a wonderful family life. Despite the periodic breakouts of their father's anger, my children had a happy childhood. Because my husband stayed gone so much with church activities, he didn't have a whole lot to do with raising the children. Mostly, as they say, they were really raised by a single parent.

As my husband began to get older, he was not having the successes that he had hoped to have as a minister. Also, as he was disappointed that the children were not falling into place for him to be proud of them, we had some problems, as all families do, and he began to get worse. Then, we realized that he was really mentally ill. I think that had been the underlying problem all through the years. I found out from his only sister that, as a teenager, he had exhibited some emotional problems. Things deteriorated and we finally did go to counseling. By then, all of our children, except one, were either in college or just out of college. We still had one young son, Mark, at home. The counselor saw my husband and me separately and together. One day, when the counselor saw me privately, he told me, "You must take your young son and leave." Since we lived in a parsonage, I would have to go and find a place to live. I was already sick with this crippling arthritis, so I said to the counselor, "What can I do? I can't work; I don't know what I can do. And my oldest child is only 23." The counselor looked at me and said, "I hate to say this, but that's what welfare is for." This came as such a blow to me. At this time in my life, I was going to have to resort to being given enough money to live on each month.

But, I did have a daughter living in Atlanta, so I came here. My daughter had just a small apartment, so we couldn't live with her. But, I managed to get on SSI, enough for Mark and me to live in a small apartment here in Atlanta. It was a sad time when I had to move out and break up the family. Even though you know your relationship is so bad that you need to get out, you just want those good times back. When you break up a marriage, you lose so many memories—memories that nobody else shares but that other person. Breaking up really robs you of the joy of remembering a lot of things. It's like it is when your last brother or sister dies when you get older, and there is nobody left of that set of people you have common memories with. As I get older, I realize how important it is to build memories. I think that is something that young people miss so often—taking the time to build some good memories.

I was only forty-six when I was diagnosed with rheumatoid arthritis and have had twenty joint surgeries in order to keep moving. Then, I was diagnosed with cancer, and had both breasts removed. One of my daughters also had breast cancer and had a breast removed at the young age of twenty-seven. We've had a lot of very hard things to deal with, and, all the time, I was struggling to make a normal kind of life for my youngest child. He had learning problems, but it was before all the emphasis on learning disabilities, and there wasn't too much help for him. His teachers would say, "He's just lazy." They said he tested out to have a good brain, so they thought he just wouldn't do the work. But I knew it was more than that. As we went through that struggle, I had to do all my work and all the driving. It was so painful with this rheumatoid arthritis; there is nothing to describe it.

Fortunately, through all the troubles over the years, somehow, I knew what was important—my six children. I have a lot of great memories. But I had one child, a son who now lives in Florida, who became a schizophrenic as a teenager. My husband's mother had also been schizophrenic.

My son's mental condition made for a lot of problems, and still does to this day. He is gradually getting worse, and for the most part, has had a miserable life, and that's a hard thing. If a child dies, you can adjust finally to the idea that he's gone, but when the child loses his mind, but not his body, it's very hard to know how to deal with that. And that's been a very sad and continuing problem for our entire family. We sometimes know where he is, and then, sometimes we don't know where he is. We don't know how he's going to react when we call him on the telephone, and we are all rather afraid to be around him; it's just that bad. He seems angry about everything and suspicious of everybody. He did good things and had good things done to him, but he can't see it. You know that's the way a schizophrenic person is, he turns and twists things into something not good.

But I came up here to Atlanta in '75, and we've had a very happy life in spite of all these other things. Now, my children are grown, and most have their own homes. Last year, my oldest daughter was the Academic Librarian of the Year in Kentucky, and my daughter that teaches school in Dekalb County was one of Georgia's best teachers in 2000. We've just all come to a very good place and I live a very happy life. But I learned a lot through those years—how to cope and how not to cope. I did not cope too well with the occasional abuse of my husband. If I had been abused every day, or if the children had ever been abused, of course, I would not have been able to stay with him. But I continued to live in that situation, thinking it was best for my children. I'm not sure that was the right decision, but we did the best we could with it. The children believed that there were enough positives in our lives, because my husband was very sweet in between his temper tantrums and abuse, and everybody that knows him from the outside thinks he was very nice. He would only lose his temper when he was just fed up with the rest of the world, and I guess he had to have a place to blow. That's what abusive people do.

Janice: How many years did you stay with him?

Thirty years, thirty years—but, as I've said, the first fifteen or twenty years, he would just occasionally lose control. The doctor thought he had a personality disorder which started in his youth, and just got worse and worse. He was hospitalized for a while and when I went to see what I could do, the psychiatrist said there was really nothing that I could do. My husband was in his fifties by then, and the illness was so deep-set, all I could hope to do was to stay out of his way. For about the next five years, his temper was really bad. It was during those five years that I got this crippling arthritis, and I think this was really overwhelming to him. I had been able to help him a lot before, but I was no longer physically able to help him. The first year, I almost had to stay in bed, and I just think he couldn't handle that. As he withdrew from me, his secretary's husband died. So they got together and he became involved in this extra-marital relationship. But I think it was only the result of my illness and his needing somebody. I was no longer able to be there for him because I was too sick.

Janice: You say he was abusive to you. Would you tell me how the abuse would take shape?

Well, in the earlier years, he would become very angry and slap me or push me. One of the worst times was when I was pregnant with my fourth child; he became angry with me when I was almost in my last month. After that time, I wouldn't tell him if I was going to stay or leave after I had the baby. So we went through three or four months when he was on his best behavior, waiting for my decision. But here I was with four small children, and how was I going to make a living for them? I certainly didn't want to leave them alone with him. So I finally made a decision to stay, and he made a lot of promises that he would not lose his temper, but it still happened a couple of times a year.

Although the children knew the abuse happened, they never saw him abuse me. But I remember those last fights were just horrible. Although it was years ago, I remember he did some of everything to me. He tried to choke me one time, until my breath was just about cut off; he shook me by my shoulders until I passed out; he spat in my face; he tore a brand new night gown that somebody had given me into shreds off my shoulders—and my shoulders and hands and everything were so sore with this disease at the time. It was almost as if he was mad at my disease, or that's the impression I had. So he became very threatening, and he would go out a lot and stay out late at night, and I would dread to hear him come in. By then, I had moved into a bedroom away from him on the other end of the house. But sometimes he would be in one of these states when he came in late at night and he would come in and sit on my bed and talk in a monotone. I couldn't even make out what he was trying to say most of the time; he was just completely out of his mind. But it was always so scary because, from that, he could've just ever-so-quickly gone the other way and become enraged. So it was a very scary time for about five years until I finally left.

It's so hard to leave when you've had a family together so long. And, of course, back then, we didn't have people writing articles about this, so I was on my own. Abuse was a thing that was hidden and shameful. Nobody talked about it. That was the worst thing that we had to do as a family, we had to not talk about it, because if we had talked about it, this would have ruined my husband's ministry in the Methodist church. So, I made some bad decisions. Today, I would make a different decision. I would say to myself, "Take your children and get out, now."

Things are so different today, and abused women should use all the facilities available to help them: shelters where they can go to and be protected until they can get established, and the counseling centers where they can go for help. I hope if there is one message that I can get out for abused women, it's this: "Get out and make a life for yourself and your children." It's just not worth it to stay with an abusive man and suffer. If you don't leave, you'll look back, like me, and regret that you spent so many years living with somebody who was so unappreciative of your efforts and so uncaring that he abused you. You'll wish you had all that time back to do something better and build something meaningful.

If the abuse starts before you have children, it's easier to get out. Once a man hits you, he is going to hit you again. I worked with the Atlanta Council on Battered Women (CBW) through the years. I couldn't get out to do much, but I called the counselors and reminded them that they were scheduled to answer the phones at a certain time. In fact, CBW gave me a Willing Worker award back in those days for doing that. I've learned a lot about people through other people's experiences and by studying abuse situations. And I have just concluded, if he hits you once, for sure he'll hit you again. So, get out. No matter what you have to do, you can exist on welfare until you can get yourself on top of things. It may be hard, but it's a lot better than putting your family through that abuse.

Janice: Do you think that there are any signs that women could look for in men that might indicate they had the potential for abuse?

You know, I looked back at that, and my children and I have talked about that. My children have said to me, "Did you see anything like this in him before you married him?" But, you know, there was just nothing. The only odd thing I can recall from our courtship is that every now and then, he would have these suffocating attacks, attacks which I now think were anxiety attacks indicating emotional/mental problems. But that's the only thing he did that was strange. At the time, I didn't know what that was, and I urged him to go to a doctor, but he wouldn't. He said he'd had those attacks for years. But now, I think he was already having anxiety attacks, and his mind was affected. So, if you see anything like that in a man you're serious about, you need to really follow through on it. I should have just insisted that he go to see a doctor or psychiatrist when I first observed this, but in those days, it was not easy for people to go to a psychiatrist. And if people found out a minister had gone to a psychiatrist, he very likely wouldn't get another appointment. It was just that kind of world we lived in. Thank God things are different now. We live in a world where people accept this. So, that was my life basically.

Janice: What do you consider to be the best invention of your lifetime?

The best invention of my lifetime? Oooh, that's an interesting question. There have been so many things, but for me probably the washing machine (laughter). With six children, I think it's probably the washing machine!

Janice: Okay, is there anything that you wish was never invented?

Hmm…. Gee… There must be something that I don't like out there, but I can't think of anything just right off hand.

Janice: What is your life's greatest joy?

Oh, my children and my grandchildren. I don't know how older people without children or grandchildren get their happiness. I just have wonderful children and that definitely is my greatest joy.

Janice: What about your greatest sorrow?

My greatest regret is having lived so many years with a bad decision to stay with my abusive husband, instead of leaving to make a new life for myself and my children.

Janice: How have the position and value of women changed over the years do you think?

Oohhh, over my lifetime I think I'm in the "transition generation." My mother was definitely in the old generation. Women stayed at home and did everything there and never went out and didn't get an education. They were perfectly satisfied with that; they never thought it should be any other way.

Then my generation came along. We were beginning to be able to get educated like men were and as easily as men could, so we could do a few things that the generations before hadn't done. But the culture had not changed that much, and so, we were still expected to do what we had always done. I only worked outside the home three or four times during my marriage. But one time, when I went back to teaching, that was when I had three children getting married in one year. We had to have more money, so I did go back to teaching at Miami Dade Community College. That's the last time I taught. But women were really expected to do everything and also tolerate an abusive husband. People didn't understand this abuse of women; so often they blamed it on the women more than they did on the man. People had the idea, "Well she must have done something to deserve it." I think this attitude made women stay when they otherwise wouldn't have stayed because they would have had to reveal the abuse, and the society was not very helpful to abused women during that time. It was very hard, and you just didn't talk about the abuse; you were really by yourself in this whole thing, except for your children.

Really, since all this happened to me, it was just in the beginning of society's concern for abused women. A Council on Battered Women, for instance, is a very new thing. So, I *really* went through a "transition age" for women, where you were neither fish nor fowl (laughter). I think it's easier for women today to do something about their abusive life than it was about thirty years ago when I moved up to Atlanta.

But, fortunately, my children and I could all talk very easily together. For instance, do you remember the book that came out *Co-Dependent No More*? My children and I studied that book; we just went through it because we knew that we had been impacted by those thirty years of living with their dad, and we were all co-dependent and apt not to make good decisions. So we just all got a copy of that book, and we'd get together and talk about it. It was the best thing we did for ourselves during that time. That book is so good.

Janice: And what do you think of the women now who are on the verge of womanhood?

Well, they've got quite a challenge. They've got a lot to work with, but they are now at the place where it's going to be really hard to break through to do more. It's been twenty-five years or so since I got out, but I think, from now on, it's going to be a little harder to push through what they call the "glass ceiling" and make more strides. We still have married the men in our society who think women are supposed to do whatever they want *and* do most of the things at home. Only here and there do you have a man that understands that if the woman works like he does, then he should take his share of the work at home. But, this is going to be the biggest battle. We still have much work to do on this.

Fortunately, I really trained my two boys differently; they cook, they know how to sew on buttons, they know how to take care of children, they love children. I look at them and I think, "Oh boy, what I would have given for a husband like that." (laughter)

Janice: Do you think it's easier to be a girl when you were a girl or do you think it's easier to be a girl now?

Well, I think it's easier to be a girl now. But a girl now, has got the really hard things to do. We've been able to do a lot of things, but, like I say, I think changing the attitudes of men will be tough. Bless their hearts, they've just been taught, and are still being taught by women that are raising them, that women have these limited roles. Consequently, men sometimes think they are something extra special and women should look up to them and look after them, and they expect that from their wives. This is going to be a hard thing to change because you don't change culture over night. We're moving, but I still think it's going to take a lot of work. It's going to take a lot of really outstanding women willing to be almost abused by society for their aggressiveness. Women are going to have to be willing to do that if they are ever going to break through to have everything a man has in this society. And, it's going to take some time. Women have got to be willing to stay the course, I think. I've had a lot of time to think about this. I can't do anything else, but I sure can think.

Janice: Do you think it's important for a woman to have a husband or boyfriend in her life?

Well, there are women who only think they are worth something if they have a man in their life, and I think that's terrible. They have been brought up in a terrible way as far as I'm concerned. We should not define ourselves by a man. It's fine to have a good man in your life, and a sexual life is a very fulfilling thing. However, women should not define themselves by whether they have a man in their life or not.

This is a battle that one of my daughters had. She's a very pretty girl and she learned that she could attract men very easily. And it has taken her half her life to figure out that she is okay without a man in her life admiring her.

Janice: Okay, what one thing do you wish women understood about life, love and longevity?

Okay, let's see. About life? We should understand always that tomorrow is another day and there is nothing that happens to us in our lives that we can't get through if we learn how to take care of ourselves. We *will* be able to do it! I had an old friend in my earlier years who always liked to say whenever something bad happened "This, too, shall pass." And I think that is absolutely the truth. We have to know that we can do it. You have to learn that early. Girls tend to think that their emotions must drive them. How they feel is the most important thing, and however they feel they have to act on those feelings. But I say no; a woman can control her emotions. Talk to yourself, reason with yourself, think about where your emotions are taking you. You have to practice saying "No, my emotions will not control me. I must think about this, I must evaluate this." I told my girls, "Talk to yourself, bring out all the sides that you can think of about this whole thing that's making you so emotional. Talk it through with yourself." They've told me that's one of the most powerful things that I have given to them, helping them to understand that they do not have to act on their emotions. You act on reason. Now, that's life.

On love, I would say to young girls, "Honey, you're going to fall in love a dozen times between now and the time you die. You have the right to act on some of them and it'll make you happy if you pick the right person. But, there are going to be times, even after you marry, that you are going to see people that you are attracted to, and you're not going to act on that because you've committed yourself to your family. If [the object of your attraction] is a good man, he won't push you any further. But you're going to fall in love so many times." We just don't fall in love one time, and that's it, but I don't think young women know that. They think there is somebody perfect for them out there, and the first one is the only one. Oh, it's such a fallacy.

Falling "in love" is so different from "loving." Falling "in love" is fun and rewarding and a wonderful thing to have happen to you when you can act on it and be involved with the person as a couple. But, love is blind. It must be nurtured continuously and it becomes such a strong support for your life when you really give yourself, commit yourself to a person, and he commits himself to you. When you build on that love and you learn that when that 'in love' feeling fades (which it's going to do at times) you'll have to work at it more to make it exciting. It's about five or six years when you begin to think, it's not quite as exciting as it used to be. But the love that you are building, by caring about each other and nurturing, just is a wonderful, wonderful thing and it doesn't go away. We should educate our girls that this being "in love" feeling does not last forever, and it can just pull you into making very bad decisions. But I don't think we teach that to our young people. They should be armed with this knowledge that there is life after this person. I want so badly for them to go into that situation with their eyes wide open. It's not to say that those feelings aren't good feelings and right feelings, they're just human nature, but those feelings should not be able to control your whole life. A lot of times, you have to be able to feel something else. Young people are going to have to exercise better judgment and think about those feelings as part of their life.

Janice: The last one is longevity.

Oh longevity. Well, I'm seventy-five years old so I guess I have it (laugher). I really never expected to live to be seventy-five, to tell you the truth, because of all the trauma of my diseases, and then I got congestive heart failure last year. I just thought I probably would not live very long. My dad came from a family of heart-diseased people, and all of them died either in their sixties or earlier; my dad died when he was 71. I always kind of thought, and with having this disease that it is so debilitating, that I probably wouldn't live this long. And I just feel every day, when I wake up, that I am so grateful for having that day. I think I'm just getting a bonus with all of these years that I really didn't expect to be here. I really expected that I would die during my sixties. But so far, so good, and I'm enjoying every minute of it.

Janice: What do you think your secret is - that brought you all the way through the sixties, now, to seventy-five?

It's hard to put a finger on that, but you know when they discovered this thing about the endorphins in the brain, are you aware? I believe that the more you laugh and have good experiences, maybe that's what keeps us going: with those endorphins being pushed out, with pleasant experiences and laughing. I have several women friends who, when we were all able to drive and able to get around in the later fifties and sixties, we used to feel free to call each other up and say, "Well I'm feeling down. How about coming over and let's just build up some endorphins?" (laughter)

But I believe it. I know that is one of the ways you have a happy older period of life. It is still having friends - new friends and old friends that I've made since I moved in here two and a half years ago. I have some wonderful friends right here. But, those old friends that I have had through the years—that could come in and we start like we were forty, fifty, years ago—I just believe those solid good relationships are the key to life. Whether they are family or friends, and they will be both, I believe the most important ingredient is friends.

Janice: I had a very very good friend, she's passed now, but whenever we were having a crisis in our lives, she or I would make a phone call. We knew when one or the other called, whatever was going on had to stop. She'd say, "I'm coming over. Do you have tissues or should I bring my own?"

That's so wonderful. You do need people like that so much, and if you have a lot of friends, you don't have to be so hard on one person; you can share with a lot of people and do that same thing. I didn't know everybody as I started doing this. Each of us brought some of our friends that our other friends didn't know, so we were old and new friends. But now, all the friends are like old friends.

There is one thing that I haven't said anything about, and I think this may be a part of building a happy life: don't count on always being able to do things. You must learn from early on to read, think about things and have a wide variety of things that you are interested in that don't require action. Because we all, as we get older, will have some restrictions. We're feeling fine and we can get out and go, and all of a sudden we can't get out and go. We need to build a happy life into our head as we go along. I was home with the children so much by myself that I did a lot of reading about a lot of things. I took advantage of friends, like a botanist friend of the family that knows many things. My children can't believe I can stay here so much by myself and never be lonely. I always have something new I want to learn about. I'm learning, now, about the history of the Arabs, and I want to find out just how they came to be what they are. I think curiosity is so important.

Janice: What is the best advice anyone ever gave you?

Well, it could be that it was Mabel with her "this too, shall pass." Her advice was usually "this too, shall pass" or "don't be anxious, be peaceful and do what you can to make the situation better." That probably was the best advice I ever had. Mabel was at least fifty years older than me.

Janice: What is it that you wish you had known then, that you know now?

That I could do it. That I could go out on my own and make it. That although it was just a little scary, I could do it. I'm not a great person for always going to scripture for things that I think or feel, but I do feel that one of my favorite passages in the New Testament would have been great support for me: "I can do all things through Christ, who strengthens me". And I could have done it. I don't believe that God necessarily comes into our lives to straighten things out. What he promises us, I believe, is to give us the strength to do it ourselves. He puts us in a world full of all kinds of threats and dangers, and he puts as much into us as we'll need to face those dangers and make the best of it.

Janice: If you had a 14 year old daughter, what would you want her to know?

The most important thing is that she is loved. I'd want her to be able to feel that through her entire being - she is loved. And whatever it takes for you to do or be what God intended, you should do and be. It's the most important thing for any of us, to know that we are loved. Not guessing or hoping, but to know it. That was the secret of my good childhood. I knew that I was loved, no matter how bad things were. Or if I did something bad or whatever, I knew that my parents loved me. There was just never any doubt.

I think that is the most important thing for any of us. We worry about so many things for our children, but if we could ever get across to them that they're loved, they'd be all right. To know that whatever happens, we love each other and will support each other is a great comfort. I believe that if we live so that our children can see that when they are little, that attitude is established for life. I didn't spank my children very much. I believe if I had to do it over, I wouldn't even do the little occasional spanking that I did. My rule was "if you do something that would be harmful to yourself or somebody else, then you have to experience some pain." That's when I spanked my children, but I don't even think that was necessary. By living and experiencing, you can just see so clearly how love can overcome any of the problems, if you start early enough. Children can really feel that love. In the teenage years, it's going to be hard, no matter what. If they have already learned that they are loved, they are not going to go too far from what you taught them. And if they go far from it, they are going to return to get some help and get through it.

Janice: Do you think you got a chance to finish all of your life's goals?

That's a good question. NO, I think I got stopped by my physical limitations. After I left my husband and started a life on my own, I was so sick that I was limited in what I could do. I really had to work with people that were right around me. I just would have loved to be able to stay at one of the houses where battered women are allowed to go, and be with them and their children and share and maybe help some of them. But I just didn't have the stamina. This is an awful disease, which requires you to rest an awful lot, so I didn't fulfill that goal. But I did some things that I'm glad I did, and I'm very proud of my family. They have given me so much more than I ever gave them.

Janice: **What is the biggest mistake that you think young women make in love?**

To think that once they are in love, that's it. They feel they have to have this person and they may never have another one. It is such a wonderful feeling and they don't want to give it up for anything. They don't want to think about it, they just want to have it.

Janice: **What advice would give to young teenagers on relationships?**

First, be a friend. Take it easy on how far you go with the lovemaking until you established a relationship. It's useless when you go the other way. Sex without friendship and intimacy is useless.

Janice: Why do you think teenagers don't listen to their parents?

It's just a part of growing up and separating. They have to separate from their parents. They all do it in one way or another. It's just that a parent has to be so wise and so careful that they allow them to feel like they are welding some power without squelching their relationship. [Parents should] just maintain that authority figure however long enough to get them through their teenage days. Talk through things with them and be there and show them a lot of understanding. Don't be judgmental. But they [parents and teenage children] are going to separate. They have to. Parents and teenage children: it's one pulling and the other one pushing, and it's just a constant readjustment of the relationship all the time.

Janice: How has getting older changed your viewpoints on a lot of things?

Experience teaches you so much. You can read about something, but you just really have to have the experience to grow.

Janice: At what age did you fall in love, and how did you know it was love you felt?

Well how far back do you want me to go (laughter)? I fell in love the first time, I think, when I was about thirteen, and I was head over heels in love. But then, that boy moved away, and I fell in love with somebody else until, finally, I was in college and almost ready to graduate from college. I met a man I had a lot of things in common with; we had the church in common and we learned to like each other.

You can't just go on the feelings of love. You must try to reason and analyze your feelings. If you're absolutely crazy about this guy, and he shows you some very bad traits, you just need to forget him. It may seem like the end of the world, but it's not. You are going to fall in love with somebody else on down the line who has good traits. Use your head. Think about your feelings. Why do you feel that way? Ask yourself if you're overlooking something. Don't deny facts that are obvious.

Janice: At what age would you advise a young lady to get married?

I don't think you can say an age. Some women mature earlier; some women have goals that they want to fulfill, and if they meet somebody before what they really want to do is done, then I say put it off and see if that lasts. If that doesn't, there will be somebody else on down the line. I certainly don't think that any girl ought to get married until she knows within herself that she is okay and that she can do anything she wants to do, that she doesn't need this person to make her whole.

Janice: Should I tell my parents that I am not a virgin and that I am currently sexually active?

I think honesty is always the best policy. A girl might be surprised at how much help she might get from her parents. If she's not on "the Pill," she might be put on "the Pill," and that would be a good thing for her if she insists on being sexually active. For some women, I'm sure it varies, but some women's hormones push them into situations. But, you should be mature enough before you do it because you know you have to take "the Pill" or some kind of precaution.

Janice: How do you cope with the loss of a lover and the loss of a loved one?

That's a hard one. That's two different things. In both cases, I think you have to grieve over the loss. When you lose a lover, there is a grief period when all your memories of the things you did together come back. With any loss, you have to grieve, I believe. It is really a double whammy when you lose both a lover and loved one at the same time, but it just means that you have to work harder to learn what you do to grieve and get through it. Time and taking care of yourself and talking to people are going to get you through it.

Janice: How do you instill, in young girls, the idea of loving themselves, so they don't look for someone else to fill that void for them?

Well, if we knew the answer to that, we'd really have it, wouldn't we? I think it starts so early. It starts when they are babies. If parents only knew what a great gift that would be to the child to help them to learn to be self-sufficient and to value themselves while they are also learning to value other people. But I think you can't start helping a girl in her teenage days to feel that valuable and confident. It has to come earlier. There is no doubt in my mind that it's a very hard job to change a teenage girl who doesn't have that. It's going to take a lot of counseling and nurturing and many positive experiences. A girl really needs to understand early that somebody else cannot always fix her [problems]. If a girl can't learn to feel good about herself until she's a teenager, then she's going to spend time looking for someone else to help her feel good about herself.

Janice: What do you think about popular culture, music, movies, videos, etc.?

Well I think it has a definite effect. We can deny it all we want, but it does. And it just breaks my heart to hear some of the lyrics that our young people listen to and sing.

Janice: Why do some parents have a favorite child and won't admit it?

A lot of things go into that. Sometimes, it's not a real situation they feel. I think some young people might feel that their parents like one more than the other, but it's not real. It may be that a young woman feels this way when the consequences of something she did makes it seem like her parents don't like her as much as her brother or sister. Sometimes, it's because she does things differently than her brother or sister, and she is disappointed with the consequences of her own actions. I think very few parents really have a favorite. I believe that if the young person could be willing to talk and express this to parents, things can be worked out. I know there are lots of bad parents out there, but if a child can't talk to a family member about these situations, they ought to go to a school counselor, because they need to talk about it with somebody. It could not be real, but if it is, then she needs to learn how to accept that.

Janice: **How do you feel that parents should help their children with peer pressure when it comes to drugs, sex and everything else?**

Well that's a big question, too. Wow. I think there have to be some basic rules in a family. Just like in any organization, there have to be some basic family rules, and I think the children need to help make those rules. I think family councils are great, wherein everyone has a chance to make and understand the rules and the consequences of breaking the rules. That's the best way for parents to get their feelings out about what they expect their children to do.

Janice: **What should you do when your mother does not act like a parent and she doesn't protect you?**

She should go seek some help. If a mother does not protect her child, that's a form of abuse. The mother needs to get to a counselor who can help her; she needs to air all her issues and feelings and find out how to protect her child.

Janice: How do you stay hopeful in a hopeless world?

Hope is always there. A germ of hope is always lying around somewhere, and you never know when it's going to pop up and say, "Here I am," so keep looking for it, and don't give up. That is a basic foundation of living life. Keep that little kernel of hope always in front of you or know it's around there somewhere. And keep on struggling through until you see that.

Janice: Out of all the periods of history you lived through, which was the most interesting?

Well, it's according to how you define "interesting." In these modern days, there is so much happening in the world: new things coming to life and new ways to do things. It's all just popping wide open everywhere. But, I think the older part of your life can be the most rewarding. I feel that during these last 25 years of my life, I've been a whole person, and that is what I want to be, a whole person. Along with all the many things that are happening, just like the "endorphins thing" we were talking about earlier, you learn so many new things and you say, "Oh yeah, that's why that happened." It's an "aha" situation appearing all the time. And, I think if you lived the first part of your life fairly well, then the older years can be the best time of life.

Janice: If you won a chance to go to congress and speak to our political leaders for ten minutes, what would you say to them?

I don't particularly want to say anything to them. I guess I wish that they could feel certain things. I wish they would think that, as a country, we really ought to treat other people and ourselves better. We don't really have to have all this war. I think we've had two great political leaders, and this may sound strange, but one of them is Bill Clinton. I was just amazed at how this man could just go to China and woo these people with kindness and no blame and could do so much just by talking to people. Oh, how we need him now. And the other one, of course, is Jimmy Carter. Carter has been able, since he was president, to do so much good for the world. His presidency was stolen from him by the Kulmani over in Iran. But, I think he has shown us how much good can come from just one person: one influential person going to these places trying to make peace. And, look at the democracy he has fostered, especially in Africa. It's just wonderful what he has done. And, like I said, Bill Clinton was a wonderful president; I don't care what his sexual habits were. I couldn't give a rip about them (laughter). Probably, the reason men were upset is because they were just jealous. They were jealous they didn't have access to women like he did. I think he does have a need for love that comes from his unstable childhood. I think he is, emotionally, a needy person. Still, he was such a wonderful president. I never will see another president like him, and he had the spirit that they all need to have. Most of the politicians have big egos, and I just want to tell them that they are really our servants. This office does not elevate you to be all-powerful. You are our servants and should act like that. I feel this way particularly about the Republicans, who do not want to share anything with the poor people. I hate the way they cater to the rich. Their philosophy just troubles me so much.

There are some times when we are under a lot of stress and a lot of the decisions [politicians] make impact so many people. And, there are times when I am by myself and I don't have anybody to talk to about it. I just really have to cut it off the TV for several hours and think about something else completely, because I want so badly for them to make a difference. You know there are people who need help, and you see the politicians saying things that show that they don't understand where those of us on the lower echelon are coming from. They are blind, so blind. Politically, as long as the Republicans stay in power, I don't think [the government] is going to do a whole lot for poor people. There are young women, single parents, who work trying to make a living for their little children and are not able to get off in time to go to PTA. Then, the car breaks down and they are completely devastated and overwhelmed. They need more money to take good care of their children, but, often, don't get any help. They get low salaries while all these entertainment people and political people keep getting richer and richer. We have things just so scrambled. We're going to have to work a lot harder to make up for the Republicans getting in power. Here we go again, back into the old routine of the Republicans not wanting to spend any money on the people who are in need, and they refusing to give poor people adequate health care.

If I could speak to the politicians, I would tell them it's so sad and so wrong that some people have so much while others have so little and have to keep on struggling. We will never live up to our dreams in America until we learn that as long as there is one person down in poverty, none of us can be truly happy. I would suggest to the politicians that what we need is a guaranteed minimum income for people so they can live like decent human beings. If people can't work, then the government should guarantee them a minimum income. I live on a very tight SSI, but at least I know I've got that, and I can plan for it, and I live perfectly happy. People need to know they can have a roof over their heads and food without constantly fearing they will have to live on the streets. When you can't buy your food or have transportation to get around, every day that happens to you, your self-worth goes down the drain even further.

So many things in this country are just so unfair, so utterly unfair. It's the one thing in my life that I don't feel that I have any ability to change. That whole thing with the Florida voting and all that, it was the minorities who didn't get their votes counted! I do think we all need to send e-mails, letters and cards to our politicians in office to let them know what we're thinking. I wish we had more people doing that.

We have no justice in our society because the poor people are not equally represented under the law. It's so obvious, and I can't see why we don't do something about it. Our society is never going to be what it should and could be because we are not seeing to it that justice prevails.

Janice: What influence, if any, do you think the church has on this issue?

I think churches are so sterile. I don't know about the black churches, but the white churches are just so sterile. I think if all the lawyers in the Methodist church would get together and just donate a tenth of their time to the poor people, that would be more worthwhile than their money for our society. I don't think a person's role in the established church is the basis for deciding if the person goes to heaven or hell. I believe it is how you live your life. I have become so absolutely discontented with the church. Not that I don't believe in God, I just don't find a place in society to go gather with other people that makes it feel like it's expressing our faith. It's gotten so that I just can't discuss my faith or my beliefs with those church people anymore. What they talk about is so unimportant. And, I don't want to waste what little time I have left talking about those insignificant things. It doesn't bother me that I don't go to church, and nobody really cares because I can't give them any money and I can't set any tables or cook any food for them to eat. The [people in the] church just seem to serve each other all the time. That's not for me. I struggled against that for the whole thirty years I was married to a Methodist minister, but we had some high moments, where we thought we were doing something.

Back in those years, I stayed home most of the time, and mothers did a lot of activities in the community. We don't have that anymore, unfortunately. The premise of our society today is things and more things. Most people are out there scrambling to get more things. The people on the bottom are scrambling to make a basic living, but even the people in the middle class are scrambling to get all those extra things that they see advertised on T.V. and just can't live without. But when they get these things, they're still not satisfied.

I tried, for so many years in the church, to get the women who have their circle meetings every month to reach out and help. Some churches had maybe 10 or 12 circle meetings every month. I used to try so hard to get them to meet once a quarter, and then in the meantime, donate some time to help out in the community. I would make long lists of suggestions, but they didn't want to do them. For example, I suggested going down to see what's happening in our courts, to see who was getting justice and who wasn't, and then, during that one quarterly meeting, share what was learned with the others. This would have been such a broadening experience. But, all they wanted to do was eat dinner or have little finger sandwiches and gossip and plan the next big meeting they wanted to have at the church. They just didn't respond.

I remember when we came out with the big civil rights thing in the sixties, the Methodist church changed the proclamation of civil rights, and I taught a class. And even though that didn't go far enough, at least it was taking some steps forward. We had such a wonderful response to that. I remember the first day that we did it, it was supposed to be over at 11:30, but when it got to 11:30, some of the young women didn't want to stop, and they began to go to the phone and call people to pick up their children. I saw new ideas and people breaking through old assumptions and understandings. Every now and then, you would have something that would provoke some concrete action like that, but it was so seldom that you would have such a breakthrough. That was a turbulent time in the church: ministers, in general, being out front trying to motivate people and changes. A lot of the churches were very divided over the civil rights ideas, especially in the South. It was a very turbulent time for being in the ministry. When they let my husband stay in the ministry after all this fall out, the bishop said to me, "Well he could have sued us because we promised him a job for coming to the ministry".

There were thirteen ministers that year that got into trouble. And, every one of them was a case of mishandling money or finding someone else they'd fallen in love with to run around with. I wrote a letter to every person that went to the next general conference, but most of them weren't punished in any way. I also wrote the conference a letter about my family and what we experienced with my husband; in my last sentence I said, "When I die, let the honest homosexual bless my bones," because that was when the homosexual issue was so big in the church.

Someday, I think we're going to look back at how we've treated homosexual people and we're going to be so ashamed of ourselves. Just like we looked back in shame on slavery. It's been found that the homosexual man has a brain very much like a woman's in size, shape and color. And one day, we're going to regret that we have treated these people so horribly over something they had no control over. I got off on a tangent, didn't I?

Janice: I'm glad that you say that the questions were worthwhile.

They were, they were. In some answers to the questions, I could've just go on and on. They were big questions, both yours and the girls. Good questions. And it's too bad that girls and mommas and women, and men too, don't just get together and discuss those questions a lot. I think that would be such a help.

Janice: I think so too, and I think this is going to be such a help to the girls to hear your story.

I do think this is a good project. I liked the idea when you told me about it, and I told my son and my daughter that live here, and I said I'm just fascinated to hear the questions, and I think it's such a good idea because we waste so much of our wisdom in this culture. There are oodles of women who could do the same thing I'm doing this afternoon; maybe they would answer these questions a little differently, but they could contribute so much.

Lessons from Louise

Silence is not golden; it can be deadly.

Abuse was a thing that was hidden and shameful. Nobody talked about it. That was the worst thing that we had to do as a family, we had to not talk about it . . . Things are so different today, and abused women should use all the facilities available to help them. I hope if there is one message that I can get out for abused women it's this: "Get out and make a life for yourself and your children."

Never allow an abusive habit to form.

Once a man hits you, he is going to hit you again. Regardless of what he says, he'll hit you again. It may take months or even years, but he'll hit you again. I've learned a lot about people through other people's experiences and by studying abuse situations. And, I have concluded, if he hits you once, be sure he'll hit you again. So get out. No matter what you have to do . . .

It doesn't take a man to make a woman.

. . . There are women who only think they are worth something if they have a man in their life, and I think that's terrible. They have been brought up in a terrible way as far as I'm concerned. We should not define ourselves by a man. Its fine to have a good man in your life, and a sexual life is a very fulfilling thing. However, women should not define themselves by whether they have a man in their life or not.

Love can be a fleeting thing.

Honey, you're going to fall in love a dozen times between now and the time you die. We just don't fall in love one time and that's it, but I don't think young women know that. They think there is somebody perfect for them out there, and the first one is the only one. Oh it's such a fallacy. . . We should educate our girls that this being "in love" feeling does not last forever, and it can just pull you into making very bad decisions. But, I don't think we teach that to our young people. They should be armed with this knowledge that there is life after this person. I want so badly for them to go into that situation with their eyes wide open. You can't just go on the feelings of love. You must try to reason and analyze your feelings. If you're absolutely crazy about this guy and he shows you some very bad traits, you just need to forget him. It may seem like the end of the world, but it's not. You are going to fall in love with somebody else on down the line who has good traits. Use your head think about your feelings. Why do you feel that way? Ask yourself if you're overlooking something. Don't deny facts that are obvious.

FAVORITE BOOK

Codependent No More by Melody Beattie

Discussion

1 . **Are there any signs that might indicate you're with an abusive person?**

    A. What is an abusive relationship?

    B. Are there different kinds of abuse?

    C. What are some of the stages of abuse?

    D. What might be the first clue that you're in an abusive relationship?

    E. What steps could a young woman take to remove herself from an abusive relationship?

    F. What are some of the agencies and governmental entities that might assist someone in an abusive relationship?

2 . **How would you identify someone who might have abusive tendencies?**

    A. How might he behave?

    B. What factors might he want to control in his girlfriend's life?

    C. What should you do if you begin to see abusive tendencies?

    D. Who should you tell if you're being abused?

3. What things make a woman a woman?

    A. What do you believe a woman must possess in order to be happy?

    B. How do you define success and failure for a woman?

    C. How do you define success and failure for a man?

    D. How do these definitions differ?

    E. Is it possible for a single woman to be happy and fulfilled and alone?

    F. Is there anything wrong with the above scenario?

4. How do you recover from heartbreak?

    A. When did you first believe you were in love?

    B. What was the outcome of that situation?

    C. How did you get through it?

    D. How did that make you feel emotionally?

    E. How long did it take you to get over it?

    F. Have you believed yourself to be in love since?

    G. Do you think it can happen again?

5. What did you learn from Louise?

A. What did you like about her?

B. What didn't you like?

C. Was there anything you didn't understand?

D. Is there anything you'd ask her for clarification or regarding a subject not covered in the interview?

E. What else would you like to know about her life?

F. Are there any points that you disagree with her on?

Write a message to Louise in 100 words or less.

The soul would have no rainbow if the eyes had no tears.
--Minquass Proverb

Audrey Brooks
The Quiet Storm

During my interview with Louise Strickland, she stated, "there are plenty of women right here is this building who could do what I'm doing right now." I knew that Louise lived in a retirement facility, which was brimming with possible interviewees. After I completed her interview, I asked if there were any women that she could suggest that would be interesting to interview. She recommended Audrey Brooks, one of her neighbors across the hall. She said she would discuss it with her and then give me a call. Ms. Brooks agreed to do the interview. I told her briefly about the project and scheduled a convenient time for her interview. When I met Ms. Brooks, I was surprised again; she was another one of those women, who looked like she had found the fountain of youth. She didn't look like she was 70 or even 60. After, I had spent a couple of minutes with her; I coined a phrase to describe what it felt like to be in her presence. The phrase is "the quiet storm." This phrase came from a radio program that I used to listen to; it consisted of jazz tunes and music that seemed to relax and quiet your spirit. Ms. Brooks has a quiet sophistication that puts you at ease in her presence. She is not the least bit stuffy, but 100% sure of herself. Her manner is quiet and controlled, but also very powerful and self-assured. She is able to draw you into her world and paint word pictures that make her story come alive before your eyes.

As the interview progressed, I learned that Audrey had survived heartaches and disappointments that you would not wish on your worse enemy. Her mother died, when she was three, she was sent to live with various relatives, she got married and divorced very young, had one son, whom she adored, and he was murdered senselessly on the streets on Washington D.C. She suffered discrimination on the job and a myriad of other heartaches that would have been the excuse for many to quit getting up in the mornings. Yet she rose above all of her misfortune and decided to live life on life's terms. She does not complain about how cruel life can be, instead she embraces her misfortunes and finds joy in her journey.

I could not believe the blessing that I had been given to be able to interview her. She is quite impressive, she has a way of making you feel at ease and she was very comfortable being interviewed. Her mannerisms and style made you forget the camera was there. The interview was very conversational; she did not have any apprehension answering any of the questions. Being in her presence was comforting and I didn't want to leave. After the interview, she showed me pictures of the people and places that we had discussed in the interview and she gave me a wonderful gift, even though I should have been the one to give her a gift. She gave me a beautiful plant that I admired in her apartment. I know her interview will inspire you to be a better you. If you listen to this interview with an open mind, there is a lot to be learned about surviving life and triumphing over whatever circumstances life presents you.

Audrey Brooks

Audrey. . .

My name is Audrey May Vivian Trust Tiggs Brooks. (laughter) Trust is my maiden name my birthday is April 11, 1925. I was born in Washington D.C.; 2315 Virginia Av. NW. The house was right across from the place that Nixon made famous, the *Watergate Hotel*. When I was three years old my mother died, leaving my father with 5 girls. I was the youngest. My oldest sister was 17 years older than me, so by the time I got up to be 4 or 5 my sisters were leaving home. I do remember my oldest sister, Virginia, we called her Virgy, she took me to a Naval Base, that's where they were inoculating little kids before they went to school. The man said, "stick your arm out," and he stuck me. I yelled; I was thinking to myself now it doesn't hurt that bad, but I'm supposed to yell, because I'm a little girl, so I yelled. But it wasn't too long after that my sisters moved out that my dad got his sister, Lenore, who didn't have any children, to keep me and my sister. After I grew I realized it was a pretty upper-class neighborhood because they had a car, and there were only two people on the block that had a car and one was a doctor. My aunt worked for the government. And my uncle Hardy had a barber shop which was downtown on 11th St. in Washington D.C. I think he had three or four barbers in there, which was unusual for a black man to have a business in that part of town. I stayed with them until I was

10 years old.   It was when my grandmother, who also lived with my aunt, passed away that my aunt decided she didn't want girls in the house after school by themselves. Not that we did anything, but that's the way she felt, so we had to move out. My sister and I were split up. My sister went to go live with one family and I went to live with another. It was all right; everyone treated us fine. So I stayed with Mrs. Milburn until I graduated from junior high school, and by that time, my dad got a job working for the government. But in those days a black man working for the government was manual labor.

By the time I was getting ready to go to high school, my dad got a house, 401 Tea Street, NW, which is down the hill from Howard University. I stayed there and graduated from Armstrong High School. I did not go to college, even though I was valedictorian of my class. I remember the night that I came off of the graduation stage, after I said my valedictorian address, I just about died doing it, but I made it through. My teacher came up to me and congratulated me and handed me this paper that said I could go get a job at the government. All I had to do was show up; it was called the Federal Work Agency, the FWA, and now its General Services Administrations. My teacher gave me the name of the person to see. I went down there, of course I had to go, because in those days you didn't say 'no' to things like that. So I went down to the Federal Work Agency and they put me in an office as a typist. I had learned to type, so I stayed in there I guess six months in that particular office. They didn't really have much for me to do; I copied things out of the register and so forth. Finally another job came about in another one of the offices there. They sent me over there, and there was a gigantic machine; they called it a listing machine the pre-runner to computers. You could put figures in and it produced results. I learned how to use the machine. It was intimidating at first, but I did it. I went thru the government like that, I went from one stage to the other, they called them grades; you went from grade 2 and 3 and 4 and five and you keep on going.

I had a boyfriend named Chester all the way through high school. He went to one high school and I went to the other. I graduated a half year ahead of him. I was 17 and he was 18, and we decided that we wanted to get married. It was around the first of September, which was a holiday, so we didn't have to go to work that Monday. So, my older sister, another lady and my dad took us to a minister and we got married. At first they thought I was pregnant, but I wasn't. There was no way in the world I was going to do that to my dad.

I wanted a baby. I remember when I was 10 years old living with my aunt, I was down in the basement and I had a baby stroller, baby carriage. It was one of those big old ones, you don't even see them now, but my doll babies were in there. And I remember I was playing with these dolls down there and I remember saying a little prayer to God, "Please let me have a child when I get grown so I will have somebody to love." And in ten years, I had my little boy, Chester and I had been married a year and a half. That was good. But the marriage didn't last, so I went back and got a job in the government. My son and I made it from there. I was able to put my son in nursery school, because this woman, her name was Senator Margaret Shay Smith, worked to get these little nurseries, about 4 or 5 of them, around the Washington area. They were for low-income parents. Even though, I was working for the government if I took home $65 dollars a month. I was doing good. The teachers really worked with and taught the children in the nurseries. So, when my son got into kindergarten, he was advanced. I was so amazed I would say "Oh my son is in school now, he's going to school." When he came home from school, I'd ask, "Well what happened today?" He was so disgusted he'd say "We didn't do nothing but play." Then they sent me and two other mothers, we'd all been in this preschool together, a letter. They wanted to get permission, to take our kids to another school where they were doing testing. If they passed these tests they would put them up another grade. We were really anxious about that, so I remember taking my son to the school where they had the tests set up, and he passed so they put him in the first grade. So I'm excited about this too. Here's my son, he's gone and skipped kindergarten, so he got up there in the first grade. After awhile, he started having headaches. So, I said to him, "Nathan, is everything all right at school?"

He said, "Yea mommy."

I said "Is anyone bothering you?"

He said "There is this one boy named Butch."

I said "What is he doing?"

And Nathan said, "He's telling me I have no business in that class that I'm supposed to go back to kindergarten." (Laughter).

I said "Really."

He said "Yea and he pushed me,"

I said "Well okay well you're gonna have to tell the teacher that Butch is meddling with you."

He said "But he's bigger than me."

I said "Look, mom has to go to work I can't come up to school everyday to see about you and this kid. Now if he's bothering you, you supposed to tell the teacher."

And he said "Sometimes we're out on the playground or whatnot."

I said "Well okay, if he comes up and pushes you again, then you push him back, and if you see a stick or something you pick it up and hit him. And I said "If the teacher calls and wants me to come, I will come, don't worry about that."

He said "Okay."

I guess it went about a month or whatever, maybe not that long. I asked him, "How's everything going with you and Butch?" And he said "Oh we're friends now!" (laughter). He must have whacked him one. He said, Yea he came and pushed me one day and I pushed him back." So that was the way he went thru, even high school. Every time he got into a scuffle with someone he would make friends with them. He told me "You know, Momma, the way you can keep peace with somebody is to make friends with them." We need him around here now.

He went to Winston Salem State College and graduated, in '66 I guess. Next summer he'll be 51 years old. My dad also died in '66. So when Nathan came back to D.C., I decided to renovate my dad's house and give it to Nathan. He lived there with, Bernard, one of his cousins. He worked for the National Institute of Health. I went by the house often to see how they were doing. They never knew when I was going to show up, and see what was going on at the house. They took care of it, because I told them if I saw something, a beer bottle or whatnot, "You guys have to move out." They said "Oh no, no no, no, no, we're going to take care of it." And they did. I mean, I didn't get the kind of negativity that I hear people talk about.

It was in March, I went up there on a Saturday and Nathan wasn't up there. He was at a play area where he had gotten a job. There were young teenagers there, he was coaching them. I said "Well what are you doing out there on a Saturday?" He said, "Well we're working on these skits and we're going to be perform them next week." Nathan said, "I came out here so we could go thru some of these things today, so we'd be ready for next week." He said, "I'm so hungry, Momma, can you bring me something to eat." I went and got him a chicken box and I took it out there to him. I sat in the car, tooted the horn. He came on out and I handed it to him and he said "Oh thank you, Mom." And I smiled at that because he'd stopped calling me "Mom" 'cause he thought that was too childish. He started calling me Audrey (laughter). He said "Thank you, Mom" and he went back in, and I felt so good with that. I mean that just went all through me, you know, having him call me "Mom" again.

That night about 1:30 in the morning the phone rang, it was Bernard. He called and told me Nathan had been hurt. I said, "What do you mean, hurt what?" I asked "where is he?" and he told me Nathan was at the hospital. I called a cab. I didn't think I should be driving. It was Palm Sunday; I thought I should look decent if he's in the hospital. I put on a suit and I had on my coat and hat and everything, and by that time, the cab had not come, so I just got in the car. I couldn't wait any longer.

When I got to the hospital there were police there. The police were there along with Bernard and Glenn, his two buddies, who were in the car with him. Glenn had been driving one of those little small cars, and these two guys had been following them real close. These two guys kept running up behind them real close. At first they thought it was some guys they knew, but then they looked around and realized they didn't know these guys. But they kept following them. When they stopped at the light at 7th and Tea, the Howard Theater was there. The guy on the passenger side got out of the car and walked towards the car Nathan was in. They said "Well wonder what this dude wants?" So Nathan was on the passenger side, so he got out to see what he wanted... and the guy killed him...one shot. There were people who were standing out on the corner when the car stopped. They witnessed the whole thing; they got the license number, the tag, so the cops were able to pick him up.

At the hospital there were all these detectives, and cops were there and they were getting ready to come to me, and I said "Don't come to me just stay away." Finally they came back and they said "We have to take you downtown, we have to get more information from you." So I went. But in the car, I started to talk. I said, "Okay I know that you all are probably thinking this is a young black man who's out here partying." I said, Well that is not the case." I just went thru the whole thing. He just got his degree and blah, blah, blah, blah. I just felt like I had to defend him because I know how they think about young black men. They didn't say anything they just went through the whole thing.

So then after a couple of weeks, I went back to work. I think I stayed one day. We were having evaluations and my new supervisor gave me a poor evaluation. I said you've got to be kidding, I mean I had always gotten top evaluations because I was a good worker, and I was getting raises and everything else. So then I took off and I went to my doctor. I told him, "I'm tense." And he said "Well what happened." So I told him and he said "You should have been here before now." He gave me a prescription, and he said "First of all, I don't want you to go back to work for thirty days, you need to stay off, and take this medicine." I took thirty days, and before the thirty days were up, my girlfriend's boss called me. He knew about my son and everything else. He had left the agency and went to work for the Peace Corp. as one of the directors. He said "Well Audrey, what are you going to do?" I said "Well I don't know, but I'm going to get out of the agency, I can't stay there much longer." He said, Well "I tell you what, I'm going to give you the name and address of somebody, to go down to the Peace Corp; maybe they can give you a position overseas or somewhere, they can tell you."

So I did. I went down to see this man; he was from an African nation. I talked to him, and I could see his purpose now and his situation. He could realize I wasn't ready to go anywhere. I was just not ready, so I didn't get that job.

A girlfriend, Helena, who went through this whole situation with me, said "My friend and I are going out to California, why don't you come on and go with us?" I said, "Well okay, that's fine" I went and I decided that's where I wanted to move, because I needed to get out of D. C. So that's what I did. I decided to move the first part of August, and by the end of August I was out in California.

I told my sister where I was going and she said "I want to go too." I said "Well okay, you do what you got to do." She came down and helped me pack, and I went out there and I got his house. I called my sister, and I said "You should see it, it is so nice and in this beautiful neighborhood." So anyways, wasn't but long before she was out here too. (laughter) And that has always been the case. She is five years older than me, but she follows me. (laughter). She follows me.

I realize now that, I've lived so much longer and gone through a lot of changes, God was with me. I know now that if there is something that you want to do or if you need some direction, the answer is to turn within, to the God place in yourself. And you will get the direction you need, and all you got to do is follow it. And that's what I've been doing. You have to have trust and have faith in yourself and what you can do. I didn't expect to be president, but I knew I had enough of whatever I needed to get the kind of job I wanted, in California, and I did.

Janice: The first question the girls ask is, How can I show my mother that I am very responsible so I can get out of the house more?

Okay I'm trying to think about that. In the first place, why isn't her mother letting her out? Does her mom think she's too young to be out there? Where is she trying to go? This girl should know that her mom knows that there's stuff going on out there and she should realize her mom loves her enough to want to keep her away from anything that might be harmful to her. Anything could happen with young kids out at night, and her mom is trying to protect her. Her mom is expressing her love by trying to protect her child. Tell her it's not anything that her mom is trying to hurt her with. If her mom didn't care, she would let her go and do anything she wanted to do. But because she loves her, she wants to keep her safe.

Janice: How can I get my mother to talk to me more about her life, and what's going on in my life?

Well it's probably some things that her mom hasn't been able to deal with herself yet. She has to realize that if her mom is going through some bad times or whatever, she will need time to be able to clear her system. She probably doesn't want her little girl to know some of the things she's had to go through. But in time, I don't know how old this child is that's asking the question, but in time, if she lets her mom know that she wants to know, she'll have to be patient and they'll have time to sit down and talk.

Janice: At what age did you fall in love and how did you know it was love that you felt?

I still don't! (Laughter) Oh shucks. Fell in love. I'm trying to think, how did I meet Chester? Okay I'm going to state it this way. It was infatuation. Love is something that goes real deep, you can meet somebody and you get all bubbly and right away you think its love. It's not necessarily love, its infatuation. As time goes on you'll learn the difference.

I was out of high school, I was 17 and Chester was about 18. He was the only young guy in my life. And we used to go to the movies, because that's what we could do back in those days. I guess I thought it was love because no one else came into my life, and we did a lot of talking. It wasn't done like it's done now. You just didn't move in, and say: "Well we're just going to move in together." Chester and I had a good relationship. I'd met his mother and gone through all of the formalities. In time we decided we wanted to be away from our parents, not that they were giving us any grief, but we wanted to be independent. So after high school, we both got jobs, and it was time to get married. I guess we figured that was love. So that's what we did.

Janice: Do you feel as if you got a chance to finish all of your life goals?

I still have plenty of time. I've thought about that. So far, I think I've done pretty good. I know I've done pretty good. But I will complete more goals.

Janice: How do you survive the lost of a love?

I think about my son a lot. But I don't mourn him. I miss him an awful lot, but to mourn is to put a brick there and you're gonna hold that for the rest of your life? No, In fact, whether you believe it or not, I had moved up to another little town in California called Rona Park. I was pretty depressed up there, not daily but every once in a while I'd come down with a lot of depression. One day I was sitting in this big chair, I used to sit in. I was in the fetal position and I looked up and there was my son. And he walked in and he said "Mom what's wrong, you feeling bad? What's wrong?" I said "Oh no, I'm fine, I'm okay, I'm okay" and he looked so good. And he held his hand on his stomach. "I said what's wrong with you?" and he said, "Well I got a little belly ache." Where I was living, there was an upstairs. Being the mom, of course, I said "Go on upstairs to the bathroom" and he looked at me and he laughed and he went on upstairs. This was 5 years after I had left D.C. after he had been killed. And all of a sudden it seemed like some kind of transition went over me and I knew I had to go back to D.C. I had to go back because my niece was there and my sisters were there.

And I figured it out. Nathan was showing me that it was time to let go - release and let go. And I couldn't wait to get back to D.C. I was calling up there and packing and I was sewing. And I felt so good to be going back because I was releasing him. See when I said go on up, I realized it meant not necessarily Heaven or whatever, but to a higher estate than what I was holding him back. I was also holding myself back. When I said, "Go on up to the bathroom," that just released me, so people when they hold on they think they have to hold on. My sister in Philadelphia was telling me umpteen years ago that she knew a woman who worked with her who had a daughter to get killed or died in southern California or somewhere down there. She had the funeral in Philly. But for whatever reason, she had the body transported down to L.A. and it was put in a glass casket, and every year she'd go back and mourn over the child in this glass casket. That's about as sick as anything I've ever heard, but people do what they want to do and how they want to do it, but she just wouldn't let it go.

Janice: How do you survive the loss of a romantic love?

It's been so long since I had a boyfriend, male friend or whatever (laughter). First of all, when things don't work out, you feel very sad because someone doesn't like you the way you like them. But you cope by deciding, "I am worth more than he is." If it is something that you can change, and both of you want to put the effort into the relationship, fine. But if not, don't hassle over it because it's a waste of your time.

Oftentimes, some guy that you figured loved you, didn't call or didn't come by like he said he was going to. You found out he has another woman, maybe two or three, and two or three babies somewhere. That's when you have to make a decision that, "I am worth more than he is." You discover all these things were going on, and you thought that the situation was one way, and you found out that it was totally different. It is time to stop focusing on him and put all your energies back into you and what you want. Everybody has some potential somewhere, so try and find out what it is you really like to do and focus on you.

Janice: Okay, Next question, what is one of the biggest mistakes you think young women make when they fall in love?

Allowing a guy to get too close and use them too much. Be careful of someone that comes around once in a while, telling you a whole lot of "baby baby" stories and all this kind of stuff. It goes back again to what I was saying – the word "love" gets thrown around too fast and much. That's what's happening with these young girls, now they're thinking they're in love and these guys are out there with two or three other women. Sometimes they know about the other women. Other times, they let these guys beat up on them and everything else. Yet, they say, "But I love him." How can you love somebody who mistreats you? What you're saying is "I don't love myself." You can't let someone walk all over you and love yourself; it's impossible.

The Bible says, "Love your neighbor as yourself," which means you have to love yourself before you love anybody else. There is no way in the world that you can love anybody or anything, unless you know that you are worthy of somebody else's love. So that is what you have to do first. Whatever you put out there, you're attracting that to you anyway. So if you're putting out some real love, you'll get some real love back. You don't have to worry about is it real or not, or is this the right person. Spend some time loving and learning about yourself. Think about little things that you could do, that you would never even think would be worth anything. It doesn't have to be any grandiose thing. What do you like to do? Do you like to paint? Do you like to write? Do you want to read? If you like to read, then go to the school or hospital and read to a child that can't read. There are some little things that you can do that really are bigger things that evolve into even bigger things.

Janice: What advice would you give teenagers about relationships?

Love yourself, love yourself, feel good about yourself, think about something that you want to happen in your life and go in that direction. You'll find that when you're doing that, you'll draw to you all the good things that you want in your life. And if it doesn't come right now or tomorrow, don't worry about it; it will come. It's on its way.

Whatever you think you want, that you're praying for, just know that you'll have it and you'll have it. You might not have it right now, but it will be coming. If you get ready for it, it will be ready for you. So take your time and don't be in a big hurry. Go ahead and find out what you can do. Build yourself up; get ready for your career. Do that first. Get your thoughts focused on what you can do and accomplish your goals. You'd be surprised how things work out. I'm sure of it, because I lived it, but you haven't had the life experience to know that yet, but it will come. Try it and if it doesn't work, then try something else and don't be afraid, because there are so many things out here you can do.

Janice: Why do you think teenagers don't listen to their parents?

I have no idea. Maybe sometimes the way the parents speak to them. Some of these parents are so young themselves, they can't pass on what they have never gotten in the first place.

Janice: How has getting older changed your viewpoints on many things?

It's made me realize that I am whole, perfect and complete. I'll say it that way. There are always things to learn. There are some 95-year-old ladies who live in this building that you can sit and talk to all day long; you never get through learning. You never get to the point where you figure you know it all. No way in the world could you know it all.

So you go from day to day and you cruise along and when things come across your path in your lifetime you try and deal with it. I wonder how is that supposed to go, what am I supposed to do with that? And either you try to figure it out or you leave it alone until you get a little glimmer and say, "Oh that's what that's all about," and you pick it up and you go from there. But don't get too tense about things. Some people have high blood pressure and other things, because they allow themselves to get too intense.

Janice: How do you eliminate or reduce stress in your life?

You pray and you know that God is with you all the time. I have very little stress in my life. Whatever is going on, you just have to release it and let it go. If you can't change it then why hold on to it? Let it go? That may sounds trite, but step by step know that each day is going to take you away from that situation. If it comes back, then you have to find another way of dealing with it. Keep on trying and just know that you can do it. Change things where you can and let the other stuff go.

Janice: How do you instill in young girls to love themselves so that they won't constantly have to look for someone else to it?

It's a spiritual thing. If you come from a home where there is no spirituality, and there was no one to guide you in that direction, then you'll have to learn it own your own. It's hard but not impossible. I would tell them to focus on their own good qualities and know their own worth.

Janice: What advice would you give a single mother raising children?

Try to do what's best for the child in all circumstances. Have rules for every age group. And know that, if you treat your children in a respectable way, they will treat you the same way.

Janice: As a black woman how do you deal with racism in America?

I don't allow it to bother me at all. Because I know I am whole, perfect and complete as I said before, and I don't go around worrying about what people might say or think about me. I just carry myself as well as I possibly can. And that's what you can do. That's all you can do, if people want to be racist that's their ignorance. There is no way in the world that you can change anybody unless they want to change themselves.

Janice: What do you consider to be the best invention of your lifetime?

The washing machine (laughter)

Janice: Is there anything that you wished had never been invented.

No, I can't think of anything not really.

Janice: Okay, what do you consider to be your life's greatest joy?

My son.

Janice: What do you consider to be your life's greatest sorrow?

The loss of my son.

Janice: When you look back over your life, is there one thing that you did or did not do that you wish you had?

No not really. I know more now about the spiritual part of life. And it's just so wonderful; really, to know that you are not alone even though you are physically alone you are never actually alone. Like I said how my son came back, my mother has come back to me too. I know I'm surrounded, and sometimes in this apartment when I first moved in here, it felt like it was full of people. (laughter) It's amazing to me, I laugh because I know it's real. It's unbelievable it really is.

Janice: How has the position and value of women changed over the years?

Oh my God, it's gone sky high. It's terrific the way women have been able to elevate themselves. The first thing I'm thinking about is in the political scene, we see step by step women are just moving right on up. It's wonderful. Condoleezza Rice, she's a black woman. She's got one of the top positions. It's been wonderful to see and it should be encouraging to all these younger women who realize that if you want to you can do it. I keep on saying it, but you can do whatever you want to do or believe that you can do. Know that not just believe, know it. Get whatever you need so you can keep on going.

Janice: Do you believe it was easier to be a girl when you were a girl or do you believe it's easier to be a girl now?

It seems to me, I don't know. I don't know about being easy. When I was a girl, there were certain things that you just didn't do. There is too much sexual stuff going on. And I don't say that to be a prude but there is just too much out there for me. And it certainly is not stuff that was going on when I was coming up. There were girls who were getting pregnant and having babies but not to the extent that they are having now. I'd rather have been a girl back when I was a girl even with losing my mother and everything else I would not be in the situation that some of these girls are in now.

Janice: Is it important for a woman to have a husband or a boyfriend in her life?

It is not important but it's a good idea. If you meet somebody who is going to be the right person for you, then that's great. Don't just settle for a husband or a boyfriend just because you're lonely or he's nice looking. Those things do not guarantee he's going to be somebody that should be in your life. He could be somebody who will use or abuse you. Don't be one of those women who are just excited to say "I got a man" you don't need that. (laughter)

Janice: What one thing do you wish that young women understood about life?

I keep going back to this spiritual thing, because it seems to be missing in the lives of mothers and daughters. Whatever you call God, it's not a fictitious kind of thing; it's not wishy washy it's for real. Everything is connected to a source that has control of everything in a very good way, in a very wonderful way actually. Whatever you need to do and whatever you need to know you can talk to God and get the answers.

Janice: What one thing do you wish women or young girls understood about love?

Well first of all, we keep talking about love being the main thing the solid thing, but before you get to love you have to get a deep feeling an emotional feeling inside. It's not like you meet somebody today and tomorrow you're in love. Love at first sight is very rare believe me. Love is something that grows step by step. No two people are going to be exactly alike it's no way in the world that's possible, but you have to find common ground to live on. Sometimes, when girls and women think they are in love, they can't see the other person's faults. Don't be blinded and don't expect anybody to be totally committed, just because you feel that way. They may not feel it in exactly the same way. Eventually that feeling you call love is going to wear off and then you're going to be stuck, if you haven't found common ground.

Janice: What is your secret to longevity?

Health! Good health. Take care of yourself.

Janice: What do you consider to be your recipe for fulfilling life?

I've been able to let things go. Knowing that life for me is whole, perfect and complete is fulfilling. I don't expect life to be anything that's going to cause me to be stressful. Knowing I am where I am supposed to be is fulfilling. So the thing is to be able to live the truth and know the truth. And don't get steered away from your truth. Sometimes people will try and take you away from what you consider to be true. So give a lot of thought to what life is for you, not what someone else thinks life should be for you. Everybody has to go their own way. Not knowing their own selves is why people get so many wrong ideas and go in so many wrong directions.

Janice: Is there a book or something that has really changed your life?

One book, it's called *The Master Speaks* by Joel Goldsmith. This was years ago when I first left D.C. and went to California, I was looking, for the right path for me. At that time it was in the 60's or the early 70's and there was so much going on spiritually. It was the age of the psychedelic stuff. I was going to the fortunetellers and all that stuff and everybody was telling the same thing. Then one day, through the mail, I got information about a book club. I love to read. They give you a list of books you could order. And I saw a book by Joel Goldsmith and I didn't know a thing about Joel Goldsmith and the book was called *The Master Speaks*.

So I sent for it, and when I got that book and I started to read it just seemed like it just slowed me down like every word was just going into me. And I said, "Oh my God, I wonder where these people are?" I'd love to be able to find these people so that we could be together. And one Sunday morning, I was in San Francisco but I wasn't going to church, because church wasn't doing a thing for me. I was an Episcopalian before I left D.C. and I joined an Episcopalian church in California. I'd go there and what they were saying wasn't hitting me it wasn't doing nothing. So I said "There's no point in me going to church, I'm not trying to prove anything to anybody." People think you should go to church. They ask, "Did you go to church today?" When you say "No," they reply, "What you mean you didn't go to church today?" Well that's your business, if you want to go to church fine.

But anyway, on Sunday mornings, I found a radio station that had the Gospels – I love Gospel songs. So I turned on the Gospels and this particular Sunday morning, I turned it on a little earlier. And this man came on and said, he was Dr. Joel Griffith and he was speaking on the Science of the Mind, and then he went on to talk about the metaphysical thing, and I said, "Oh this sounds very interesting." I said, "This is what this book is sort of talking about." On the broadcast they mentioned the name of the church. So I said, I can find them in the phone book. And right then everything started turning round for me. When the people are ready the teacher will come that's right.

Janice: What is the best advice anybody ever gave you?

I don't know, I'll have to think about that one

Janice: Imagine that you had a 14-year-old daughter and you're on your deathbed what you tell her is going to make the difference between whether she survives or not. What are you going to tell her?

Well in the first place, I don't know why you have to wait till you die to tell somebody something. You start teaching your children from the day they are born. At that point, I'd tell her to find someone she can talk to, an older woman who has had some background with children in her age group. Like this lady I know named Ms. Moss who is sitting here right now. (laughter). I'd tell her that she may have hard times, and when she does, she needs someone she can reach out to.

Janice: What do you consider to be the best way to raise children?

With good rules, back to my son, when he was in, I'll say high school. He was always out with the boys and I was a single mom, and there were certain rules that I had. On weekends if he went out with his buddies, he had to be in the house by 11:00. I remember one time I think he was a junior in high school and he went up to somebody's house, they were having a birthday party or something that night. He was supposed to be home by 11:00. I'm sitting home at 11:00 and he's not opening that door and I'm wondering what's going down here. And the phone rings and there he was, saying "Mom, they're getting ready to go over to so and so's house, can I go?" I said "if you don't get over here in 5 minutes, boy I'm going to break your head open." (laughter). I realized I was so upset because first of all he's ignoring my rules, he knows better than that. As a parent, you don't know what's going on and you don't want him out to late without supervision. So I said "you better be home in 5 minutes." I was so mad, and I said I was going to spank this guy, beat him.

I told him what I expected and it never seemed to be a big problem with him. Some of his buddies would come and ask me, "Ms. Brooks what should I do about so and so" and I'm thinking, "You should be talking to you mother." But apparently, you couldn't talk to your mother so you came to talk to me. And that's what they did. And I guess that made Nathan feel really good to know that his friends could come and talk to his mom. I wanted so badly to talk to these mothers but I didn't know them personally.

You start lovingly giving the child disciplinary things that you want them to do, when they are very young. Give them rules to follow when they start looking around and touching things, don't say "no" but you tell them why and do it with love. You have to have love along with your discipline otherwise you haven't done a thing. When you have a child and it's growing up 1, 2 or 3 years old, by the time it gets to be 3 years old you should have set down some rules. And children 3 years old now are smarter than they were when I came along believe me. You don't wait until they get 10, 11, and 12 years old to start telling them how to do something. You see that's too late. That is definitely too late. Also know that, disciplining your kid doesn't mean you have to spank them and beat them all the time. Just say things in a way that they will know you mean them.

Janice: How do you keep yourself motivated?

I'm trying not to be so motivated (laughter) I'm serious
because around here there is something always going on. I'm
a member of a line dance group, we don't have as many
performances as we used to have but it was real interesting
and real fun. But it gets to be a point now where I am almost
ready to quit. There gets to be a point in life where you say
"no," enough. I don't want to be too busy. I'm a retired
woman. (laughter).

**Janice: Tell me a little bit about your religious or spiritual
beliefs.**

I am a member of the Trinity Church. In San Francisco when
I first got involved after I found out what the name of the
church, from the Sunday broadcast. I looked in the yellow
pages, found it and went. When I arrived, "I knew I was
home." I just knew before anything was said or done it was
just a feeling that I knew that this is where I'm supposed to
be. And I was there for 22 years before I moved out here.
And I got deeply involved in that church. I went to the
classes got to be a practitioner and did all kinds of volunteer
stuff.

**Janice: What do you think the solution is to young peoples'
problems?**

I don't know if there is any concrete solution. If they are able
to find somebody that they can talk to or relate to that relates
to them whether it's the 100 Black Men or someone at one of
the Y's. There are different people who are ready and able to
talk to them and steer them in the right direction, but they

have to seek out the help they need. It is important for young people to know that they have someone who loves them. You can rattle off a whole lot of rules and regulations to young people, but if you do it without love and commitment it won't make in difference.

Janice: Imagine for some reason you have been selected to talk to the political leaders of our nation and you have 15 minutes to tell them whatever is on your mind. What would you tell them?

Well, I would talk about the children and literacy. We need more teachers, number one above everything else; we need to put the children first. Number two, we need to release the hatred and join our hearts together, in a spirit of love. We need to reach out to some of these peoples in other countries, whatever their background or religious beliefs. We should not try to change them just because we think that we are the biggest and greatest country in the world, that's part of our problem. They were saying back in WWII "Go Home Americans," they couldn't stand us because they thought we were too arrogant. America should try not to be Mr. Big all the time. As a country, we should be able to work with other countries and see what they need and see how much help we can give. If you help people in a certain way, then they will know that you care about them and we won't have all this trouble and all this war and hatred that's surfacing. We can't change people, they believe what they believe. Think about what is going to be healthy for our country and for our children, and for everybody that's concerned. We shouldn't always act like a bully. All people are connected, whether you believe it or not.

Every time other people or nations do something we don't agree with, we can't automatically say, we are going to have a war. How in the world are we ever going to be peaceful if we never extend peace? And as long as we keep on saying, we got to go to war, we got to fight them, then they're going to fight us. Then we're going to say they're bad people or worse than we are. But, we are the same way and they hate us, and it's going to go on and on and on. We have to be peaceful; otherwise, we can't expect other countries to be something that we're not.

What is that song, "Let there be peace on Earth and let it begin with me." We don't need a whole lot of grandiose talking. If we say we want peace enough and believe it enough and live it enough; it's going to change the world. Whatever century whenever it's going to be I don't know. I'll look back down here and see you guys (laughter) and see ya'll working with it.

Janice: The end

I enjoyed this, I'm glad you came.

Janice: I'm glad I came too.

Lessons from Audrey

*When it comes to romantic love, decide who is
most important in your life.*

First of all, when things don't work out, you feel very sad
because someone doesn't like you the way you like them.
But, you cope by deciding that, "I am worth more than he is."

Keep your eyes open for relationship contradictions.

When you discover all these things (other girlfriends,
children, broken promises, lies) were going on and you
thought that the situation was one way and you found out
that it was totally different. It is time to stop focusing on him
and put all your energies back into you and what you want.
Everybody has some potential somewhere, try and find out
what it is you really like to do and focus on you.

*How you love yourself is how you teach
someone else to love you.*

The word "love" gets thrown around too fast and much.
That's what's happening with these young girls now they're
thinking they're in love and these guys are out there with
two or three other women. Sometimes they know about the

other women. Other times, they let these guys beat up on them and everything else. Yet, they say, "But I love him." How can you love somebody who mistreats you? What you're saying is "I don't love myself." You can't let someone walk all over you and love yourself; it's impossible.

Know what form a fulfilling life would take for you.

So the thing is to be able to live the truth and know the truth. And don't get steered away from your truth. Sometimes people will try and take you away from what you consider to be true. So give a lot of thought to what life is for you, not what someone else thinks life should be for you. Everybody has to go their own way. Not knowing their own selves is why people get so many wrong ideas and go in so many wrong directions.

Love must find common ground in order to thrive.

Love at first sight is very rare believe me. Love is something that grows step by step. No two people are going to be exactly alike it's no way in the world that's possible, so you have to find common ground to live on. Sometimes, when girls and women think they are in love, they can't see the other person's faults. Don't be blinded and don't expect anybody to be totally committed, just because you feel that way. They may not feel it in exactly the same way. Eventually that feeling you call love is going to wear off and then you're going to be stuck, if you haven't found common ground.

FAVORITE BOOK

The Master Speaks by Joel Goldsmith.

Discussion

1. **When you are in a relationship whose needs come first?**

   A. If that relationship ends, how do you handle it?

   B. What is compromisable in a relationship?

   C. What is not compromisable in a relationship?

   D. What do you do if you are asked to make a compromise that you are not comfortable with?

2. **Have there ever been instances when you were lead to believe one thing and it turned out to be different?**

   A. How can you recognize relationship contradictions?

   B. What do you do if you discover major contradictions?

   C. What constitutes a major contradiction or a minor relationship contradiction?

   D. Can you trust someone who misleads you?

3 .   **What does the phrase, "you teach people how to treat you mean?"**

> A. In the past how have you taught people to treat you?
>
> B. What is unacceptable relationship behavior for you?
>
> C. How do you teach someone to treat you with dignity and respect?
>
> D. Have you ever accepted less than you deserved?
>
> E. What was the outcome when you accepted less?
>
> F. Do you regret accepting less?
>
> G. What steps can you take to make sure it doesn't happen again?

4 .   **Have you ever been steered in a wrong direction?**

> A. At the time did you know what you were doing was wrong?
>
> B. What was the result?
>
> C. How did you feel about it?
>
> D. Will you allow it to happen again?
>
> E. How will you avoid it?

5 .   **What is common ground in a relationship?**

> A. How can you find common ground?
>
> B. What does it look like for you?

C. Is it important to know what you need before the relationship starts?

D. What would you do if you found yourself in a relationship with someone who had goals, morals or ideas that are not compatible with your?

Write a message to Aubrey in 100 words or less.

The artist must be the medium through which humanity expresses itself.

- Romare Bearden

Lois Coogle
The Artist

When I told Myrna about the interviews I wanted to conduct, she agreed to do the interview and instantly told me that she knew someone else, Lois Coogle, who would be perfect. She said she really admired her and knew that she was a very intelligent woman with a lot of wisdom to share. Myrna told me that she was an artist and it happened that she was having an art exhibit that weekend. Myrna took me to the art show and introduced me to Lois. It was very interesting to see some of the wonderful pieces that she produced. There were painted stools, tables, platters and bowls in wonderful vibrant colors. When we found Lois among the crowd, she was looking for her shoe that she'd taken off during the exhibit. The shoe sat next to a little stool and there was a lot of laughter because everyone thought the shoe was a part of the display.

What impressed me at our first meeting was how young 86 had gotten. She was darting from one familiar face to another, telling about the inspiration behind some of her artwork and introducing old friends to new friends. She was incredibly active. We talked briefly about the interview and I told her I would call to schedule it. When the day, came for the interview I got lost looking for her home. I drove by it several times but it sat up on a hill and I couldn't see the house from the street.

When I finally arrived, Lois was waiting for me in the yard. She gave me a quick tour of her studio then we settled down for the interview, and I was amazed at her stories of cross country travels before there were any interstate highways or hotels. I was awed by all the wisdom she had to share. Her answers were poignant and thought provoking. She brought and aspect to the project that I had not considered and I don't think that most people spend much time thinking about the future, what will getting older bring? How will I maintain personal fulfillment at age 60, 70 or 80? What can I do now that will prepare me for other phases of my life? These are things that the girls needed to think about, they are also things that women in my age group need to consider. I hadn't given much thought to it until I met Lois. But, I can tell you since our interview, I have given quite a bit of thought to aging, and growing old without being "too old to breathe." I was really enamored by the ideas Lois brought to the table. I was impressed from start to finish. Lois is quite insightful and I enjoyed every second of her interview.

Lois Coogle

Lois. . .

I was born and grew up in Kentucky and had wonderful, loving, generous, kind parents. Of course that was definitely depression years. I was born in 1915, so by the time I was in high school we were having what the country called the "worst depression." My immediate family did not feel it because my father worked at the Post Office, and the government kept their employees and kept their salaries.

Probably the most outstanding and unusual thing that my family did was take long trips. In 1932 I graduated from high school, and for a high school graduation present my father thought of the idea of going cross-country. It was unheard of. There were no roads to speak of; there were absolutely no motels and few hotels across the country. I really don't know what prompted the idea, except that we loved to camp out, so he said it shall be a camping-out trip across the country.

As I mentioned, he worked for the government so he had three weeks vacation. He took the end of one vacation period and the beginning of the other and he had six weeks. We had a Model T, and we all piled in it and went cross-country. This was really a kind of a surprise because my mother had an almost pessimistic outlook on life. I thought,

"She's going to worry about this," but she went right along with the idea and enjoyed the trip.

So we'd pull up to a place, get out and ask the owner if we could camp-out in his pasture or in his yard and, of course, made friends all across the country. This was most unusual. I have one brother who is a retired oral surgeon. We both had privileges all through our lives. We went to college when our friends couldn't go to college. We did have to go to municipal college because of expense.

I had a very privileged wonderful childhood and a lot of fun. My parents were so loving and kind that they took in my mother's sister and five children, because her husband turned out to be no good. After five kids, you find out that he's no good. (laughter) We helped them. They did not live with us, but close to us, and it became a very close relationship. To this day my cousins refer to me as, "almost a sister," We helped them financially and in every other way we possibly could. So my childhood was wonderful.

In 1936, I graduated from college with a degree in Math and started working for the State Board of Health. In 1938 I went to Johns Hopkins, on scholarship, for training in Bio Statistics. I worked at the State Board until 1940 when I got married.

While I was away at school, my husband-to-be was transferred to Atlanta with the telephone company. That's how we happened to come to Atlanta, and lived for a year in an apartment. In 1942 we found this place up for sale, a four-room house with five acres. It costs less than our first automobile. (laughter) We've been here ever since. Every time we had a kid, and we had five, we added another room.

So it's been a wonderful place to raise kids and to live. And we are hoping we can be here the rest of our lives.

Your question a few minutes ago was, have I always painted, and the answer is, no. I have always been interested, as my mother was, in crafts and craft ideas. She was very good, first of all, with sewing, which I don't like, and also with making craft items. When my husband was in the Navy during WWII, I was privileged to go along and we lived in San Diego, California. After being there several months I found out that I would not know whether he was coming home that night, a week later, or when. By now, I had a baby and I was homesick and not very good company. My husband said *"Get into something, or go home to your parents."* I said, "What I always wanted to do was take art classes." I didn't take art in college because I had to be practical. I had to take courses that would prepare me for working. So I went to San Diego Community College for two years and took water color classes. I almost haven't laid down a brush since then. It was almost as if this is what I was born to do.

It was a very exciting time. We came home in 1946 and a few years later I found out that I really needed to make some money to help with household expenses, and by now I had two girls. And I knew I could never sell water colors because you have to be outstanding to sell them. So I shifted to oils and decorated furniture. First, just to make old things that we had go together. So that was the beginning of my so-called tole, T -O -L –E, which is a decorative painting. And that was the beginning of learning that other people wanted furniture, accessories, plaques, trays, etc. painted and decorated.

I had the idea of having a show each fall (this year, because of our family show, was the first time I've missed having my own show in 43 years). So that was how I got most of my orders. I was very fortunate that was at a time we needed money. We needed a lot. I had 5 children, 4 girls and one boy, and I painted all the time I was raising them. I stayed at home of course. And I was not only helping at that point, financially a little bit, but it's the most wonderful thing that could have helped me for old age. I don't have any spare time (laughter), I am busy. I found out teaching is very satisfying. I have taught thirty years and I am now teaching at Benson's Senior Center, and hopefully helping some seniors take care of retirement. So, it's been quite satisfactory.

Obviously I'm a projects person and my husband is a projects person. So when he retired, he built a shop and I took over all of the basement. We see each other for lunch. Unfortunately he's still thinks wives should fix their husbands lunches. (laughter) Sometimes I don't agree with that.

But that's pretty much where I am today. We've had a full life; we have done a lot of traveling. In 1959 we made the trip to Alaska with five kids in a white station wagon for two months (sigh). Every day, I thought there has to be a better way to have a vacation. But anyway, it was a wonderful trip. The kids still refer to it. Lee was two and a half years old and he thinks he remembers it every step of the way. Of course he's remembering what we talked about all the time (laughter). But we've done quite a bit of traveling. After our kids were gone, we joined the Friendship Force. We've been to Korea, to New Zealand, to Soviet Georgia, though it's an independent state, to Europe and to Brazil. These were wonderful trips, staying with host families.

Our kids are 3 in the Atlanta area and a daughter in Oregon for 20 years (I don't think she's gonna come back to Georgia). But we're together, all of us, two times a year. Our son is in the Washington D.C. area. And they are all wonderful, loving kids.

Janice: Any artists in the bunch?

Yes - in fact the show that we recently had was a family show. Our middle daughter is a professional calligrapher. Our fourth daughter is a botanical water colorist, and also a writer on garden subjects. Our granddaughter was in the show, and really, for her age, is an outstanding photographer at school in Savannah, working on her Masters.

Janice: The first question is, how can I show my mother that I'm very responsible so that I can get out of the house more?

Obeying her mother explicitly. There is nothing more frustrating than a mother expecting a child at one time, and he or she is 2 hours late. She will earn more freedom by following the instructions that her mother has given her, even though you don't agree. If she is assigned cleaning out the closet, make sure that it is thoroughly cleaned out and not just a few pairs of shoes moved out.

Janice: How can I get my mother to talk to me more about her life?

That is probably a very difficult question for somebody whose life was not a happy life. I can easily talk about my life because I had such a wonderful life with two sets of wonderful grandparents. I can also see if there were times when maybe you were hungry and she just doesn't want to bring it up. I feel certain that if her life, the mother's life, had been happy and satisfactory, she would want to talk about it. And I think probably she did not have a happy life, and the questions would have to be very carefully worded not to stir up old memories. Maybe a good start would be "What did you do at my age?"

Janice: At what age did you fall in love and how did you know it was love that you felt?

That's an interesting question for me because I dated my husband seven years off and on. And frankly, never at any one point thought, "This is the guy." It just sort of moved in that direction. And I knew we were coming along together, and incidentally I am very much against pre-marital relationships. And I think love is probably being comfortable with the person you have chosen and not a thing that's going to hit you overnight. I was 25 when I got married.

Janice: Do you feel you got a chance to finish all of your life's goals?

Oh no, never, never. I had ambition a long time ago that by now I'd have a school for teaching people how to paint. But so far, I don't have a school. I'm still working on it. But I feel like you always have to have something to look forward to, in learning. And I have done that through the years. Even with my children, I managed to take classes in order to be better as a painter and teacher. You have to keep moving.

Janice: What is one of the biggest mistakes you believe that young women make?

Not preparing for becoming old. I'm sure I had the same thoughts. I'll never be that old with wrinkles. I just won't let myself. Surprise!! You do get old. And it has been almost shocking to me that I go along thinking, I'm doing pretty good. Suddenly one day, I look in the mirror and I'm covered with wrinkles. It seems you move along, and then suddenly... Like when you're young, suddenly one day your petticoat is too short, or suddenly your hair needs cutting. And that is the way it's been with getting old. Suddenly you're an old woman.

Janice: What advice would you give young girls about relationships?

Well, I guess the best advice is to know there are two sides to every question and to listen to the other side. You can still get aggravated, but it's easier if you do not think. "I'm right." Take time to consider if this could have happened differently than you thought. I guess listening is the best advice I can give. But, it's awfully hard to listen when you're good and mad.

Janice: Why do you think that teenagers don't listen to their parents?

I think that probably it's the parents' fault. Are parents interested? Do they have anything to teach? Can they converse with teenagers? Do they know what's going on in teenager world? If not, they should get with it. They should know their songs, know what they are reading, know where they go. And then you have a common ground to talk. One of the things that was probably outstanding with my family was family council, and this was an idea that we learned at PTA. We had a certain time each week when we would sit down, go over what went wrong through the week, go over when you needed extra money, etc. We chose Sunday afternoon, after Sunday's lunch, at which time everybody had to be here. At that time we took up subjects like, "What is complete honesty?" And my children still refer to it as being one of the best possible ways of learning how to grow up. If any one of my children had a project he wanted particularly to work on, that was brought up. Our oldest daughter, my oldest daughter, had the idea of buying a piece of land from us. We have six acres here. So my husband marked it off and told her how big this piece of land was, how much it cost, what she would have to borrow, how she would have to pay for it. In fact this was a lesson in real estate that you only can get when you are buying. All the kids and I learned from it.

Janice: How has getting older changed your viewpoints on things?

I don't know anything that's really changed - certainly not moral issues. I'm terribly impatient, and getting older has made me realize that this is certainly not a good trait. I'm working on it. Basically, I can't think of anything that really changed.

Janice: If you had a chance to do your life all over again, would there be any major changes you'd make?

Well, I guess I would have been married to somebody else much earlier (laughter). I would have changed husbands, which is probably one of the reasons that I said under question one of the first questions about love or love at first sight. I was not officially engaged, but we had intentions of marrying. He was an Army Ariel Photographer, who later was killed. And of course that was a very awful thing in my life at that time. It probably changed my whole life considerably. But if all events had been the same, I would do what I did.

Janice: Is there any particular age that you feel like a woman needs to be before she considers getting married?

I think it's not chronological age, but maturity age. And that happens differently with different people. I have a little granddaughter who, at age 10 - well first of all she's the third girl, and at age 10 she could run a house. But her oldest sister at 15 is a scatterbrain.

I think it depends entirely on the maturity of the person, which is different for each person.

Janice: We kind of touched on this just a little bit. How do you cope with the loss of a love?

Hmm, that's hard. First of all, I found when Smitty was killed that his friends and his pastor were a help. Those people who knew and loved him were a wonderful help. And I find that so many of my friends don't want people around. But I think people are very necessary when there is grief.

I was quite young; there were other boys and other interests, which I'm sure helped. Though at the time, I didn't think anything would help. People were a tremendous help. I was not at that time much of a reader. I had not read any books on grief. I didn't know about that part of it, but there are hundreds of books now available on grief. And when my grandmother died, one of these books was consoling.

However when old people die, I am, of course, not sure, but I think in general most people think that *"He's lived his life, he had a good life"* and there is not a lot of grief.

Janice: How do you instill in young girls to love themselves so they don't look for someone else to validate them?

Well, that's a good question because I think that we're always told not to t talk about 'I' all the time. And I think. . . Oh! I know, you have to have one interest, which is more than the average person in your age group would have. And my best example of that is when my youngest daughter was 16. She kept saying, *"I don't know what to study, I don't know what I want to be."* And about that time, I went (this is funny but it made such an impression) to Garden Club, and at Garden Club we had a 16-year-old girl to speak to us on, would you believe, on frogs. She knew more about frogs than the average person, not the average 16-year-old, but the average person. So I went home all excited and I said "Laura, what you need is to learn and do something better than the average person, then you will be called on as an authority."

And I fully believe this for everybody – you need to have one interest above all the other interests.

Well Laura said, "Mom, I don't like frogs." From that day, and she'll be 50 next June, she has not missed a Christmas giving me a frog, some kind of frog. It is a memory she has never forgotten because she came up with a wonderful ambition, and is quite an authority on plants, folklore on plants, and now has moved into botanical illustration of plants. She has published 18 books on plants and gardening.

Janice: She learned something that she knew more about than the average person.

That's right. And if everybody knows this, you can't help but be happy. It wasn't any time with my "TOLE" painting until I was called on to tell women how to paint because I had studied it. It was actually new to the general public and I was so lucky, I have it figured out that that's the reason I've been happy all my life. It wasn't being married and having a house full of kids, it was having something to do that was better than everybody else could do.

The two people you have interviewed that I know. Look at them, Myrna - handwriting analyst. She has to be the greatest, she is so cute and Dr. Leila Denmark with medicine.

Janice: Why do parents have a favorite child and won't admit it?

Um, it's natural. Look at your friends. You respond to the one that responds to you, it's the same with your children. It's pretty obvious though I don't admit it to my other kids, that Laura is my favorite. She is the one who calls almost daily,

"Are you two okay?" She's the one that says, "I'm bringing supper." I have two other kids in town that I see once in awhile by invitation. It has to be about how that child responds to you, and I don't think it's wrong. I really don't think it's wrong. It's human nature.

Janice: How do parents instill the morals and values of their childhood into their children?

Well first of all, I think morality itself has changed so much, that the generation of my children hardly knows what is right and wrong. That's not a good answer because you ought to know what's right and wrong.

But so much is accepted now that was not accepted in my day. "Pre-marital relationships" is one of the biggest. Oh boy, this is awful, rather it was in my time. But now it's unfortunately seeming to be a way of life.

So, I think it's just difficult to stand up in the face of what society has accepted. My grandsons were living with their girlfriends before they were married. But when they came to my house, No Way!! Well, they think I'm an old witch. Okay, think I'm an old witch. But some people don't like to be old witches.

Janice: How do you survive, when your mother does not want to be a mother and she doesn't protect you?

Well if you are a little child, it's awfully hard to call for help. But if you are a teenager in that kind of position, hopefully you've run into a school counselor or a Sunday school teacher - somebody who could help you. You need help is the answer. And if you cannot seek it, that is very difficult.

And of course this kind of thing that I have had no experience with, not even with a friend. But my answer would be, the child needs help, and hopefully somebody would recognize this.

Janice: What does the child need to do, in your opinion?

Well she's against a mother. She's in no position to talk with the mother or to deal with the mother. I've read some cases where the child can change a mother's opinion of life. But how old is the child?

Janice: She just turned 15.

Well she definitely is old enough to seek help. Frankly, what's wrong with crossing off a mother like that? You wouldn't keep on accepting a friend like that.

I have a friend who said her mother was no good. And when she was old enough, she left home and just cut her out of her life. Why not?

Janice: The same young lady asks: "Have you ever felt hopeless in your life, and if so what did you do?"

Fortunately, never have I felt hopeless. And of course that is easily understood with my background.

Janice: What do you consider to be the best technological invention in your lifetime?

Oh my gosh!! Not the computer!! Um, the best invention.. . .. mmm.....electricity.

Janice: Is there anything that you wish was never invented.

Television (laughter).

Janice: What is your life's greatest joy?

Hmmm... teaching people to paint. I have a scrapbook I should turn over to you, notes, clippings of how people, well the gist of it, "You open up a new world to me." And that just does something to me. It's gratifying, it's a joy, it's love. Yes.

Janice: What is your life's greatest sorrow?

I guess, and this is going to be very odd, I guess my greatest sorrow is not having a husband who is an easy communicator. This is not unique to me - I hear it from other women. There can be a whole meal, and not a word of conversation. You and I could not have lunch and just sit there. But day, after day, after day, Ken can just sit there. And I'll say, "How you like this soup?" He says, "I'm eating it, aren't I?" (laughter) When he gets up in the morning, it's not "Good morning, dear!" And I keep thinking, gee it would be nice to have somebody say, "Good morning." I think being lonely with somebody is hard. But that's so small when he's so good about so many things. He lets me be my own person, which I think is absolutely necessary in a marriage. And we've been married 61 years, so somehow we got along. But I would say that is my most discomforting sorrow.

Janice: Is there are recurring regret that you have as you look at your life?

Um-mmm, no.

Janice: How has the position and value of women changed, as you can see, over the years?

Well the position and value of women certainly has changed very much from my mother's time and my time. I think women in the workplace have hurt the children. I think definitely that has hurt because nobody can raise your child the way you want him to be raised.

Um... on the other hand, I think the fact that a woman can now become an individual is important. I think for too long she was in the shadow of her husband, and that is an advantage to what is happening now. But it's gone too far – when there are children involved.

Janice: Next question, do you believe it's easier to be a girl when you were a girl, or do you think it's easier to be a girl now?

I don't feel that there has really been a difference. And I say that from my own daughters, and I have four – and my 4 granddaughters. But it's pretty much the same as when I was in school. She's interested in boys, much the same way as I was interested in boys. Where they are different is, she would not hesitate to call a boy, and I would have been found dead before I called a boy.

So again, society has changed. It doesn't have anything to do with your question, but society changing shows up so much in the church. I lived to play tennis in high school, and in college. I didn't play for a long period of time after the kids were born, but once I got them out of the way, I went back to the tennis court. The church that I grew up in said, "You do not play on Sunday, it's wrong." When my children were grown, I went back to tennis. The tennis courts were crowded on Sunday. Society has accepted it. And I think that's the way that society has accepted so many changes that your question is hard to answer because of these changes.

Janice: Do you think it's important for a woman or a girl to have a husband or a boyfriend in her life?

I don't know anyone without one, so that's hard to answer. Well if you believe in Freud you have to believe you've got to have him. I would say it's almost necessary. It appears sex is very important in a woman's life. Being married, in my opinion, is the right way.

Janice: What do you wish young girls or women understood about life?

(laughter) Hmm… That definitely you are the one responsible for what it is. Hey, that's pretty good.

Janice: What do you wish they understood about love?

Hmm… That's a hard question. Well, I feel it's necessary and I think friendship love can be stronger than between a man and woman. I really do. I think parental love is necessary.

And though it's hard, I think a child needs to love his parents the same as the parents to love the child.

In other words, when you say "love." I don't really think of romantic love.

Janice: Is there anything you think they should understand about romantic love?

I keep thinking about a plaque I have. This will answer your question. "Love at first sight is easy to understand, it is when two people have been looking at each other for years that it becomes a miracle." Romantic love is fleeting, you can't depend solely on it. We were married sixty years last November 2000, and our children had a wonderful party for us. And the invitations read, "It's a miracle." (laughter) Isn't that clever?

Janice: What do you wish women or girls understood about longevity?

That it's happening, that you're going to get old and you need to make some preparations for it. First of all, you need constantly to be aware of good health. If you can stay in good health, you've got it made. But when everything starts breaking down, it's a hard life, it's a tough life.

Both of my parents died of strokes. Foremost in my mind is, don't die with a stroke. Keep healthy, do everything you can to prevent a stroke. And my doctors also agree with this, that I should watch it constantly.

So I think young girls should remember how important good health is - and good eating habits and good exercise. I'm 86,

Ken is 94; we have our problems, I don't mean that we're pictures of perfect health. But all of our lives we've been very conscious of health. I was a tennis player; it was wonderful exercise. Then after I couldn't play tennis, I walked as much as I could, which I'm supposed to be doing now, but I have a heart condition which means I can't go up a hill.

So each phase of your life, something goes, and the better prepared you are to meet what's going, the better off you are. And you sure can't enjoy life if you've fallen apart physically, so that needs to be #1 and then #2 – have an interest, a hobby, and exclude reading. Reading gets old for old people; you can't read all day long.

Have an interest that you can pursue to take care of hours that are coming. Of course reading is important and should be included but not exclusively.

Janice: What do you consider to be a recipe for fulfilling life?

Keep healthy, keep busy. Have a reason for getting up in the morning.

Janice: I want you to think back and tell me the best advice that anybody ever gave you.

I'd rather you ask my son that. (laughter) He has an immediate answer. He got in trouble for talking too much in school, so I turned him over to his father who said, "Just remember, in life keep your mouth shut." A math teacher I couldn't understand, I guess it was astronomical astronomy, I would go back to Dr. Moore for his help and finally he said to me "Sometimes people reach a limit of their intelligence."

(laughter) I burst out crying, but I'm still remembering that. But, my best advice was from my father, who showed me that you can't hide a lie.

Janice: Is there one particular book that you've read that you feel like has changed your life?

Tale of Two Cities, oh I love that book. There are dozens, hundreds of characters, and they were all connected. There is such a wonderful picture of how they were all connected. I think it's the greatest book ever written. I just wish everybody had to read it. I'm not sure it changed my life, but it helped my thinking about relationships.

In fact, I became very fond of Dickens. In the last few years I've really gotten more into reading than I have for years. Last summer, just passed, I read only biographies, and that was so great.   Henry Ford, Thomas Edison, Lindbergh, Martha Berry, who started the school for under-privileged in Rome, GA – all exciting people, with history woven into their lives. I had a good reading this summer. You think, well okay, when you get old you're going to read. Of course you will; you'll do probably more than you have time now. But my friends, who have nothing else, have eye trouble, and they get tired easily. You need something besides reading.

Janice: Is there anything that you know now, that you've learned now, that you wished you had known 20 years ago, 30 years ago, or 40 years ago?

The importance of patience, I'm a "let's do it now!" person, and my husband is the world's most patient person. Hopefully he has helped me. I'm working on it.

Janice: If you had a 14-year-old daughter and for some reason, either death or whatever, you had to leave her and you had to leave her alone and you know that she would have very little help, what would you tell her that hopefully would prepare her to navigate the world herself?

Hmm...... 14. You don't want her to contact friends.

Janice: For whatever reason she is going to have very little help.   She's basically going to have to remember your words, and your words are going to have to inspire her to go on.

She's got to have a goal. She's got to have something to look forward to, and every day she must work towards that goal. If you know where you are going, you're going to get help - get it? But if you don't know where you're going, you're just lost. So you've got to have a goal. And I don't care if it's, digging ditches. You have to have help on how to dig a ditch, how to get a job digging ditches. You need a goal and you need to do everything you know how, to get to that goal. Now along the way, you can find out it's not a good goal, so you change your goal, but you still have to have a goal. And I firmly believe that even though it changes, you've got to know where you're going.

Janice: In your opinion, what is the best way to raise children?

Well, we as a family had so much fun. I mean giggly fun, because it's easy for me to giggle. It's terribly hard for my husband. We're opposites in almost everything. The best way to raise children is to listen to them. Listen to what they are saying – and if it's funny, laugh with them. I think laughter is wonderful. But you have to listen to the kids.

And my husband had this idea; don't say "no" to everything they ask for. Analyze it, is it reasonable? Can we afford it? What does it accomplish? Is it enjoyable? Answer all of these questions before you say no. And that makes a big difference. Some parents say "no" before the child finishes. But consider what they are asking for.

Janice: What importance has family and friends played in your life?

Oh, they are my whole life. I think friends are as strong as family. I really do.

Janice: Next question, how do you motivate yourself?

I just enjoy what I'm doing - that's motivation.

Janice: What do you feel about popular culture; you know that the music kids listen to, the clothes they wear, their general actions.

Obviously, some of it I do not like at all. The songs I cannot listen to enough to criticize them. They just don't turn me on. The clothes do not bother me, it's a passing fancy. I'm sure that too will pass. In fact, they come around to things I used to wear.

Janice: Give me a little indication of what your daily routine is like.

Well, it varies because I teach one full day, and usually one afternoon, a workshop. I get up early. I'm an early riser. My husband, at this point, likes to sleep late. So I get up, eat breakfast and leave his breakfast or indicate what's for breakfast. Then I go downstairs and start painting, unless I'm on a special project. Recently I designed menu folders for our luncheon at church – so if it's a special project, early morning is a good time to work.

Always I fill in, even with 15 minutes, I go down and paint, because I never get caught up with paint assignments. I always have something to paint for somebody. You would think that would come to an end, but so far it has not.

Special routine, I never lie down in the middle of the day, and I won't let myself read in the middle of the day. My reading is in the evening. After I do all my own grocery shopping and cooking, I do all my own cleaning. We have help in the yard one day a week. I can bring him in to help in the house. So one day a week, I would say I'm working in the greenhouse or our garden. Everyday is busy.

Sunday, I always go to church; my husband does not go to church unless it is a holiday. That's a big part of my life. I take fresh flowers every Sunday to my class because they voted to buy fake flowers, and I said, "A church is no place to have artificial flowers, they need to be alive." We do not use being old for a cop-out. "Oh we're too old," that's something I haven't mentioned. I have friends that are too old to breath, and it makes me so mad. My Sunday School class was too old to bring fresh flowers, so I said okay, I'll do it – and I do, every Sunday.

Janice: That was in fact my next question. Describe your religious beliefs, how religion has played a part in your life.

I actually go to church for two reasons. I love people, I love being with people. Second, I go to church to learn something about living. Our preacher is not teaching me anything. After-dinner speeches is what I was getting, so I quit going to church. My Sunday School teacher is a biblical scholar and is giving me what I need to study. I go to Sunday School and I go to special music programs, which I love. But, I'm waiting for a new preacher (laughter).

Janice: Imagine for a minute, that our nation decides to have a lottery to choose several citizens to sit down and spend 15 minutes with our nation's political leaders. You would get a chance to tell them your feeling about how this nation is going, what would you want to compliment them on, what you want to criticize them on? What would you say to them in your 15 minutes?

Oh I feel very strongly that there is too much government, and I am much in favor of cutting roles that hand out money. Work for it, if you want it; don't ask for it to be given to you.

I think our income tax system is much too complicated. Why can't we have a percentage across board, and cut out all this tremendous amount of time and money which it takes to come up with income tax. It's ridiculous. That almost would be my biggest concern. I don't think doing away with social security is right, but I think more attention needs to be taken on how much we pay into social security. People are just not on their own going to save, so I think much more attention needs to be put on social security than has been. A flat tax would be a tremendous help to all of us I think. Is that enough?

Janice: The last question, is there anything that I didn't ask you that you wish I had sense enough to ask you?

(laughter) I think you covered the ground. Well anything I wished you'd asked me, I could turn around and ask you. And one of the things that bothers me is why people cannot realize they are getting old. My daughters refuse to think they will ever be as old as I am. They may not, but you have got to prepare, whether you are going to get that far or not. And in general, I'm finding that people have not prepared to be old.

The fact that I'm prepared to be old is not because I'm that smart, I'm that lucky. I happened to have a hobby, an interest, that would carry me into senior citizen. I did not think that when I went to school in San Diego, *this is going to help me be happy when I get old.* Somehow we need to educate young people that they are going to get old. There are all kinds of statistics to show you're going to live to 70 easily and maybe far beyond that. So, I don't know how to do it. The people I run into now teaching at Benson have already arrived, and they've arrived without being prepared. What I need to reach are your girls. I never get calls to speak to young people; I get calls to speak to old people. That's too late. We do not use being old for a cop out. I should have been there yesterday.

Janice: I thoroughly enjoyed this interview and I'm sure my girls are going to learn a lot as I did.

Lessons from Lois

Freedom comes with responsibility

[The key to getting more freedom comes from] obeying her mother explicitly. There is nothing more frustrating than a mother expecting a child at one time, and he or she is two hours late. She will earn more freedom by following the instructions that her mother has given her, even though you don't agree.

You have to prepare for different phases in your life.

I'll never be that old with wrinkles. I just won't let myself. Surprise!! You do get old. And it has been almost shocking to me that I go along thinking, I'm doing pretty good. Suddenly one day, I look in the mirror and I'm covered with wrinkles. It seems you move along, and then suddenly you're old. Like when you're young, suddenly one day your petticoat is too short, or suddenly your hair needs cutting. And that is the way it's been with getting old. Suddenly you're an old woman. . . . it's happening. You're going to get old and you need to make some preparations for it. First of all, you need constantly to be aware of good health. If you can stay in good health, you've got it made. But when everything starts breaking down, it's a hard life, it's a tough life. The fact that I'm prepared to be old is not because I'm that smart, I'm that lucky. I happened to have a hobby, an interest that would carry me into senior citizen. I did not think that when I went to school in San Diego, "this is going to help me be happy when I get old." Somehow we need to educate young people that they are going to get old. There are all kinds of statistics to show you're going to live to 70 easily and maybe far beyond that.

In Life you must take responsibility for what you get.

Definitely, you are the one responsible for what it is.

You have to know where you're going.

She's got to have a goal. She's got to have something to look forward to, and every day she must work towards that goal. If you know where you are going, you're going to get help to it. But if you don't know where you're going, you're just lost. So you've got to have a goal. And I don't care if it's digging ditches. You have to have help on how to dig a ditch, how to get a job digging ditches. You need a goal and you need to do everything you know how to get to that goal. Now along the way you can find out it's not a good goal; so you change your goal. But you still have to have a goal. And I firmly believe that even though it changes, you've got to know where you're going.

*You must have an interest that motivates
you to move forward.*

You have to have one interest, which is more than the average person in your age group would have. And my best example of that is when my youngest daughter was 16; she kept saying, "I don't know what to study, I don't know what I want to be." And about that time, I went (this is funny but it made such an impression), I went to Garden Club and at Garden Club we had a 16 year old girl to speak to us on, would you believe, on frogs. She knew more about frogs than the average person, not the average 16 year old, but the average person. So I went home all excited and I said "Laura what you need is to learn and do something better than the average person, then you will be called on as an authority." And I fully believe this for everybody, you need to have one interest above all the other interests.

Well Laura said, "Mom I don't like frogs." From that day, and she'll be 50 next June, she has not missed a Christmas giving me a frog, some kind of frog. It is a memory she has never forgotten because she came up with a wonderful ambition. She is quite an authority on plants, folklore of plants, and now has moved into botanical illustration of plants. She has published 18 books on plants and gardening.

FAVORITE BOOK

A Tale of Two Cities by Charles Dickens

Discussion

1. **How are responsibility and freedom related?**

   A. Why is it necessary to be responsible with certain freedoms?

   B. What could happen if you utilized a freedom without responsibility?

   C. Have you ever been irresponsible?

   D. What was the outcome?

   E. Is it fair to have your freedoms limited when you act irresponsibly?

2. **How do you feel about getting older?**

   A. Do you think you will ever be as old as the women we've studied?

   B. How do you think you will be at that age?

   C. What can you do to make sure that you live to be that age?

   D. What are some decisions can you make that may limit your life or health?

E. What can you do now that will make you happy for years to come?

3 .   **Who is responsible for your life?**

A. How can you take complete responsibility for your life?

B. How can you turn your responsibility over to another?

C. Can anyone guide your life better than you and your parents?

D. Who is ultimately to blame for your life's decisions?

E. What happens when you give away your personal power?

4 .   **What do you look forward to in life?**

A. What are some of your goals?

B. What route will you take to those goals?

C. What would achieving those goals feel like?

D. What are the most frequent interruptions that keep women from achieving their goals?

E. How can you avoid those pitfalls?

5 .   **Is there something that you feel you were born to do?**

A. What gives you that impression?

B. What comfort might you derive from doing what you feel you were born to do?

C. If you haven't discovered what you feel you were born to do, how can you explore the possibilities?

D. What can you envision yourself doing in 20 to 30 years?

E. What is the first thing you need to do to get you closer to your goal?

6. **What did you learn from Lois?**

A. What did you like about her?

B. What didn't you like?

C. Was there anything that you didn't understand?

D. Is there anything you'd ask her for clarification or concerning a topic not covered in the interview?

E. Are there any points that you disagree with her on?

Write a message to Lois in 100 words or less.

Next in importance to freedom and justice is popular education, without which neither freedom nor justice can be maintained.

- James A. Garfield

Gertrude Sanders
The Educator

Dr. Sanders is the mother of one of my sisters' friends. My sister was always fascinated by Dr. Sanders, so she made all the necessary arrangements for the interview. I didn't know very much about Dr. Sanders, except she had worked extremely hard to educate herself and was very dedicated to the education of the masses. The day of the interview Dr. Sanders was not feeling very well. She had been suffering from the flu for several days, yet she decided to go on with the interview. She is an exceptional lady, interesting, funny and very dignified. Around the room were dozens of awards and plaques given to her for her community service and dedication. Dr. Saunders is very formal, but not stuffy. Laughter was very easy for her. She is an avid reader and is very sharp. Several times during the interview, she stopped to interview me on what my goals were, the work I was doing and what was next for me personally. I enjoyed her interview, she called me into accountability to the young people I was working with.

I learned a lot about determination from Dr. Saunders. She is not one to make excuses. She is an overcomer and has the kind of self-will that cannot be stopped. She got married young, had a daughter and was divorced in less than four years. A single mother with a child to care for, she found no excuses. Her daughter did not become a reason to quit, on the contrary her daughter became her every motivation to keep going. She achieved every single goal that she set out to accomplish, it may have taken her a little longer, but she simply would not take no for an answer. Dr. Saunders provided for and educated her daughter in addition to earning several degrees, including two doctorate degrees. She traveled the world and studied abroad and shared her knowledge with generations of students, from elementary school to college. She bought property and made wise investments that are still paying off today. When I think of Dr. Saunders, I think of the Nike slogan, "Just Do it." Whatever the goal, she just did it. Sheer determination is what spurred her on and I am pleased to share her interview. I know some of her determination has rubbed off on me and I hope you will allow it to rub off on you.

Gertrude Sanders

Gertrude. . .

I am Gertrude C. Sanders, from Birmingham, Alabama. I was born July 2, 1916, into a family of 3 children with my mother and father. I was reared and educated in Titusville, which is our subdivision in Birmingham, Alabama. All three of us children graduated from Industrial Parker High School. Although I was the middle child, I graduated before my sister. My mother said, "You talked too much and you skipped over classes." I should have gotten out of high school ahead of time. But nevertheless, we grew up in a family that had a strong work ethic. We were always told, "If you want anything, then you should try to work to get it, so you can hold on to it.

My father owned a grocery store which was the first grocery store by blacks for blacks in the area. My father later worked at Hillman Hospital where he was one of the chefs. My mother was a homemaker and stayed at home most of the time with the children. We owned our own home; it was the second home built in the area. Everybody knew everybody else, and every grown person on your block was just like your mama. If you did anything wrong, the first grown person who saw you did what your momma would have done. So it was a real, real community. There were no paved streets where we lived. Our store was the store, but my father and mother taught us that you "always, always work for what you want." So I learned early that there was nothing that the world owed me. If anything, I owed the world. My parents taught us many lessons, like the Golden Rule "To do unto others as you would have them do unto you." For instance, if one of us children complained about how things were divided, say a cake for instance, my mom would have me divide it the way I thought was fair. I might have one big hunk and two small ones, and after I divided it, then she would let my sister get first choice. So you learned to do things fairly and according to the Golden rule. That always stayed with me. And another thing that stayed with me all the time was *"there is no excuse for an excuse."* Because my parents always said you may make an explanation but you don't have an excuse. If you could explain it in such a way that momma would accept it then you were on good terms, but if you didn't explain so she could understand it as other than an excuse, you were in trouble.

There was no liquor or stuff like that in our family. There was no smoking, none of that because, my father said, "You learn to do those things that you will be alive to do later on and if you don't need it at the table when you sit to eat, then you don't need it." You ever see anybody around here swallowing a cigarette? You don't need it. Also, my father and mother did not believe in lending a cup of sugar or, let me borrow so and so and so. We tried to make sure that we had what we needed so if we went to the store for sugar we bought two bags so we would not run out in the middle of the month. Watching their example, I learned to buy two of everything. I always pictured I would have twins because I would buy two of everything. I learned to be frugal that way. There was no cursing, my child can tell you, she never heard me curse. I heard her cursing once and I stopped her cold in her tracks. I said, I don't know who you heard saying that word, but I know you never heard me say it. I explained that you don't have to use profanity to get your point over. I believe that. I learned all these lessons from my parents, they were not educated per say, but they were thoroughly indoctrinated somehow.

Janice: After you graduated from high school, what was your next step?

My next step was to get married.

Janice: Was that your choice or was that just the way it was in those days?

In those days you married first and then you had children, you didn't just shack up with someone, that was totally inappropriate. So, I married after I finished high school. And a year or so later, Lilly, my only child was born. I remember very vividly, once I asked momma to keep Lilly for me; I wanted to run an errand. Mama said "Are you going to work?" I said, "No ma'am I'm going out with some girls." She said, "Take your baby with you." And that was the end of that. "I knew what I had to do," Mama said. "I raised my three and you can have one, two or three and they are yours, and nobody raises your children." That taught me a lesson that Lilly was my responsibility. And I set forth to make it work.

I was divorced before my daughter was three. I went to work in a laundry because that's what I could do. I could sew; I learned how to sew at Industrial High School. In those days we used to turn the collars on men's shirts. When the collars got raggedy on one side you could take the collar off the shirt, turn it over, and re-sew it and it would look like new. When I went to the laundry, I went to sew, but by the time I left, I was running every machine in the dry cleaners. During my lunch hour, at the laundry, I would dress hair. I had learned how to dress hair at Industrial High School. I had my little stove and iron, dressing hair at 12:00. I was making a quarter a head, during my lunch hour. I worked for 50 cents a day, you hear me good. I worked for 50 cents a day. And then I made a quarter dressing hair at 12:00.

I rented a room for 50 cents a week for my baby and me. After my divorce I did not go home to live with my parents, I was grown. My daddy taught us, that when every child finished high school, decided to get married they had to leave and get a place of their own. He said, his house was just enough for one woman and that was his wife. So, my momma told me, she says, "I'll help you; we got you a room for 50 cents a week." I moved to a rented room and worked hard because now I had to take care of my daughter and find a way to move up in life. I was determined that I was going to be a teacher. I decided that when I was in the 5th grade. I was going to be a teacher. I didn't know all this was coming but I was still determined I was to be a teacher. I worked hard at the laundry and learned everything I could and after realizing my ingenuity, the man I worked for at the laundry let me have the money to go to Miles College. I went to Miles College at night and went to work at the Laundry by day. Lilly was six years old, when I saw the inside of a college for the first time. And in nine months I had earned a certificate, which allowed me to work part-time while I was in school. I was determined and I was at an age where I knew what I was going to have to do. There was no turning back I knew I had to be the best. You have to be better than the others if you intend to get ahead. My daddy taught me that.

After I earned my certificate, I was trying to get a job so, I went to see the superintendent for black folk. I told him I wanted to work. Dr. Avis said, "You don't have any kind of degree you got some hours but you don't have a degree. I got people sitting outside my door waiting for a job and they got degrees." I said, "But I want to work." And after talking with him for a little while, he said. "Oh, you've got a child." I said, "Yes, does that make a difference?" He said, "Yes and no. It makes a difference because it has made a difference in you. I'm not going give you a job because you got a child, I'm going give you job because you want to work. All those folk out there in that hall, they want a job, but you the first somebody I heard who came in here and said, "I want to work."

I got a job teaching at an elementary school. But I didn't stop going to school. I finished Alabama State University in 1949. Then I decided I wanted a house. At that time, you saved your money at the post office. One Sunday I saw an ad in the paper for a house and I went and got my money out of the Post Office and I went down and bought a house and got out of that little room.

After I received my BA, I still wasn't finished so, I decided I wanted to go to Howard University. I started going full-time during the summers. I locked up my house and I went to Howard University in 1950. I carried my daughter to Howard with me. I put her in a reading program in Washington D.C. and got myself a job working for Sandals Sales Incorporated pulling up delinquent notices and sending letters. I worked, took care of my baby and went to Howard University.

As time progressed, Lilly was ready to graduate high school and go to college. Most of my friends were sending their children to Miles College, but I wanted to send my daughter away from here to go to college. I was teaching night school and day school. I thought, "I can't stay up late in my house and come home every day worried about what she had done." Nor did I plan to stay up all night worrying myself, looking for her to come home. I sent her away so whatever she did would be history when I heard about it. (laughter) After, Lilly was in College, I decided to go to NYU.

I went to New York to finish my Masters and Lilly wanted to go to West Virginia State - I said well all right. I had been in New York for two summers. Both Lilly and I were preparing to graduate from our perspective universities. Lilly was completing her BA and I was completing my Masters. One day, I got a call from Lilly and she told me, "I want to come to New York where you are." She said "I don't want to work until I get a Masters degree." I finally said okay, and since I was graduating, I talked with the people in New York and they gave Lilly the room that I was renting. And, I went to West Virginia State to see Lilly graduate college, before she went to NYU to get her Masters. She graduated and she didn't want to come back to Birmingham, so she went to work in Annapolis, Maryland. But she didn't go until she got her Masters degree from New York University. I knew she was prepared and ready to be on her own.

I wanted more education and I also wanted to travel. And I did get to go travel; I've been on every continent. I went to Europe first to study, then Julliard College Program between

Western Europe and the United States. I got lucky and the next year; I went to Copenhagen, not knowing that necessarily this was going to lead to another degree. I was just traveling and taking a few courses. I went to Copenhagen, I went to Smith College in Europe, and I went to Boston two summers. I said I don't want to go on to school I want to go onto something new. Then, they came up with a new degree the ED.S degree.

The University of Alabama in Tuscaloosa was offering this ED.S degree so I went to Tuscaloosa with my transcripts. The advisor told me, "You have taken more courses of everything than we require for the ED.S degree. All the coursework is complete except for writing the thesis, and we cannot give an ED.S. degree just by writing the thesis. I would suggest to you that you go back to one of the schools that you have been where you have done so much work. And do the culminating project there."

Instead, I went to Atlanta. I went to Atlanta because I had relatives and we had property over there. I did the ED.S degree in Atlanta, while finishing the degree, the culminating project and writing my dissertation, my mother died. Mama died May 24th I was to graduate with the ED.S. Degree in August and I did. But, I didn't do so well after my mother died. I took some time off, but a year later I went back to Atlanta, that next summer and started on the Ph.D program. And that's how I got my Ph.D from Atlanta University. They have merged with Clark College since then and became Clark Atlanta University.

Janice: Born in 1916, what did you consider to be the best technological invention of your lifetime?

I guess I would have to say the telephone. Telephones were invented before I was born, but we didn't have one. To begin with, we didn't have a lot of things like: running water, electric lights, television and so forth. We used a well for water and lamps for lights. But, my dad had a car when I was born. He always had a car.

Janice: The next question is what is your life's greatest joy?

My daughter. My sister married a year after I did. My parents really liked my sister's husband; he was really good, really nice and a great provider. My sister had a daughter the year after I did. They had a daughter and then had a son. Because my sister and her husband were working together things were much better for them. But, I was determined that my daughter was going to get as much out of life as their daughter.

Janice: What is your life's greatest sorrow?

Losing my mother. She left me in '72 and I got a PhD in '75.

Janice: As you look back over your life, is there anything would consider your   most important regret that you didn't do or wished you hadn't done?

Well I might say I wished I had saved more money than I have saved. To leave to my daughter and grandchildren who don't want it. (laughter) I saved money, but I also invested in real estate. I bought property. My daughter gets rent from the rental properties, to this day. I bought this ground and built this house and I'm leaving it to my grandchildren. So I've done very well as far as that is concerned. I wanted to make sure that all three of them, were fortified to take care of themselves.

Janice: How has the position and value of women changed over your lifetime?

Tremendously, women are in high demand at this time. More women are going into positions that at one time you wouldn't think of. Women are living longer and staying on the job longer. One reason the age is going up is because the people now have so many things that make life easier. People don't have to do such hard work anymore. Machinery has taken over to do the work that people used to have to do, and that makes a difference. You see all these old folks now, they are staying around longer and many of the older ones are in better heath than some of the younger ones. The difference is that old folks ate out the ground. We harvested what we ate. These young folks eat out the can. (laughter) And that makes a difference. And the younger ones ride in cars, trains and buses, while older folks who are living now - they had to walk.

Janice: Do you think it's easier to be a girl when you were a girl or do you think it's easier to be a girl now?

It's difficult to be a girl now because of television. Just because of television. That's what it all boils down to. In my day certain things, adult things, were kept from children. But now you see everything on television. There is no more mystery, everything is shown on television. Another problem is that so many girls are buddying with their mommas. And the mommas are partying with their daughters, saying curse words, drinking, and so forth. Mommas want to be friends with their daughters. These girls don't need more friends; they need guidance and love from a mother. And, because mothers are trying to make sure they are friends, the daughters have lost respect for the mothers. My daughter has never seen me drink, never seen me smoke. But these girls with these young mommas smoke with them and drink with them. It's difficult for girls. I'd always tell my granddaughter, "Don't try to make your daughter grow up too fast - let her be a child as long as possible. She's nine years old, and she can fix her own breakfast and do her own hair. That's the mothers' responsibility. Let your child be a child. I never did anything around my daughter that I would be ashamed of, never did and never will.

Janice: Has there been a book or an event in history that has changed your life?

The book that changed my life was by Carter G. Woodson, *The Miseducation of the Negro*. I can't tell you why but it really set the pace for me. I was going to night school, working day and night, and Dr. Hayes was one of my teachers and he assigned that book to me one night, and he said come prepared for class the day after tomorrow and discuss it. I read that book I analyzed the book and learned from it. It helped to shape who I am.

Janice: Do you think it is important for a woman to have a boyfriend or a husband in her life?

Yes, I feel that a woman should have a husband or boyfriend in her life. Think of a market basket, most of the time a market basket got two wide hooks. If you take the market basket and fill, it and took hold of the two wide hooks, and tried to carry it by yourself something is going to fall out. It's hard to manage by yourself. But if you took the same market basket, then fill it with something and you took one side your friend or your husband took the other side the two of you could go on down the road. If you try to handle both sides by yourself what's happening to the basket. Something is falling out; maybe the load is too heavy to carry alone. But with someone who is giving you the proper help you can carry the weight, keep it together and the two of you can go around the world with it. I really feel that a woman and a man should be together, and the longer you can stay in any relationship that is conducive to your getting along and getting ahead, the better.

Janice: If you could gather all the young women and girls together to explain to them about life, what is the one thing you wish women understood? First about life? Second about love? and thirdly about longevity?

First, life is so short. You ought to make the best of it as possible. And there is nobody who has come back to tell me that it's better over there on the other side than it is over here. So you have to live now. You can't put things off. You have to work and make your goals and not live life talking about "one day, I'm gonna." I do believe that.

What I want women to understand about love is that love cannot be bought. You can be happy and love in a two by four house, if all the other ingredients are there. And you can be unhappy in a millionaire's house if that's all you're there for. I want women to understand that love is what love does. If you say that you love me and I'm naked, barefoot and hungry and you don't do anything about it, you are a lie. Love is what love does, remember that. I believe in that.

As far as being able to live a long life, part of it is hereditary and the other part is environment. When I say heredity makes the cup, environment fills it up. I have lived longer than my mother, longer than my father, longer than my sister, longer than my brother. I had good genes, but I added to that by learning to live healthy, I never smoked, I never drank. I worked hard, educated myself and took care of my child. I've lived longer because I chose a healthy lifestyle that promoted longevity.

Janice: And your secret to longevity?

Like I said, my secret is to take care of myself. To not abuse myself because really and truly, my father died at age 61 my mother died at age 78 my sister died at age 64 my brother died at age 70, now at age 87 my time has been up. I try to take care of myself. I don't drink I don't smoke and I don't take medicine unless I absolutely have to.

Janice: Is there anything that you wish you knew then that you know now.   That if there is one lesson that you learned that you wished you had known that lesson 50 years ago or 60 years ago o r 70 years ago.

I'm not sure about that one.

Janice: What is the best advice that anyone ever gave you?

The best advice I was ever given was to be true to yourself that's the best advice, to be true to yourself.   And, if you don't talk too much you won't have too much to take back.

Janice: What do you consider to be the recipe for a fulfilling life?

I always try to remember to live by the Golden Rule, and the Ten Commandments. And I remember to count my blessings one by one. I can't think of anything else. Count your blessing is a big one. Then you'll realize you are so blessed. When you have problems, you are not the only one. Everybody has problems and your problems aren't new. There is nothing new under the sun just a different way it was put together. You can't have a problem that somebody else hasn't already had one like it. That's one thing, when I was counseling, I always told my counseling students, you didn't invent this problem, and it's been there.

Janice: What do you consider to be the best way to raise children?

I just told you by the Golden Rule. "Do unto others as you would have them do unto you." That's what I would always tell my little girl. "Do unto others as you would have them do unto you. And remember if you point your finger at someone, you have three fingers pointing at you so treat people like you want them to treat you. If you want people to be your friends, then you have to be one. And if you have an enemy, do something to make a friend out of it."

Janice: How do you motivate yourself?

Reading, I keep a book on a nightstand. My sight is getting bad now, but I still read. I like to read books of vocation and books of wisdom. And I read most anything I can pick up.

Janice: What advice if you had an opportunity to sit down for 15 minutes and talk to our nation's political leaders, what would you tell them?

Number one, do like the Boy scouts; be prepared. Be prepared emotionally as well as otherwise. And be prepared prayerfully.

Janice: What should you do if your mother does not want to be nor does she act like a mother and she doesn't protect her?

She needs a counselor. Then she needs a mentor or somebody that's going to be with her. She needs to find someone who will do little things with, her not necessarily for her. She needs to get someone who maybe is a little older to do things with her, like a movie that is suitable for children, or a game or football game or baseball game or soccer game. She needs somebody who can provide proper guidance.

Janice: At what age did you fall in love, and how did you know it was love?

Now when you talk about love, are you talking about friendship are you talking about a relationship? Or she may be talking about lust. First of all, girls need to make sure that they know that there is a difference between lust and love. Secondly, before they start talking about love, they need to be clear about what they are looking for. They need to be honest and ask themselves, if they're looking for beauty or if they're looking for sex or if they're looking for protection, or if they're looking for something physical and materialistic; someone who gives them diamonds and they think oh he loves me. Some of the things we identify with love have nothing to do with love. Girls have to also ask themselves questions about who they are involved with. Does he love me because of what I give him? Does he love me because of how I look? Does he love me because I have materialistic things? Maybe he loves you because you have a car and he needs a ride? You have to ask yourself, why does he want to be with me? Is it love or lust, or a temporary fix to some problem or need? There are a lot of people who think they love someone because another person meets a certain need. Be honest and identify your reasons for wanting to be with this person and why that person wants to be with you. Most of the time, if you honest, you'll discover that what you were calling love is really not.

Janice: How can I open up and share my feelings with my mother?

Sit down and talk to her and be honest.

Janice: What advice would you give to a single mother trying to raise children?

I was a single mother from three years old until she got grown and I'm still a single mother. Be the mother. Through the years Lilly was not treated wrong, I never got married again, after my divorce; I put all my thoughts into her. I had very, very good men friends. Now that has been a good thing too, but I know I have not been a straggling mother. Before anything else, I was a mother and I always remembered that the men friends in my life were friends and they were good, but I would not allow anyone to come in and run over my daughter. I bought all my stuff myself. And I recognized that Lilly was my responsibility and it was up to me, to see after her. I was always Momma.

If you want to know how to raise children, watch the birds. They go away and they bring food to the babies. And then the time comes they teach them how to fly, they must leave the nest. We had a bird nest in our plant on the window. And they had two eggs they were morning doves, we watched them hatch, we watched them till they flew. When the mother bird thought they were ready to fly, she came and picked them up, then she dropped them and the momma bird picked them back up and helped them until they flew away. We watched them all the way from eggs till they flew away. Help your children but be a mother. Say what you mean, mean what you say.

Janice: This is my last question, you ready? Okay! Is there anything that you wished I had asked but I didn't that you want to spend these last minutes telling me about. Something that you might have neglected to tell me at first. Or you thought I would have enough sense to ask you but I didn't.

Let's see. Oh, well you did not ask me, about my religious faith. I am Catholic. We were Methodist and Baptist, but I became Catholic because of my daughter. Lilly is Catholic because when she was a little girl I carried her to Washington School to put her in kindergarten, and they would not allow her to be enrolled. I had to work. After they wouldn't take her in school, I didn't know what to do. As I was walking back to work, I met a nun, and we got to talking and I told her that they wouldn't take my child into school and she said, "Put her in kindergarten with us and we'll take care of her."   They took Lilly into the Catholic School, and that's where she went all the way through, High School. They kept her, fed her they took care of her. They helped me when I was struggling trying to make it. And so therefore, I became Catholic with her. My greatest love is my daughter.

Janice: I want to tell you what a pleasure it has been to share your story.

Lessons from Gertrude

Excuses are not to be tolerated.

There is no excuse for an excuse. My parents always say you may make an explanation but you don't have an excuse. If you could explain it in such a way that momma would accept it, then you were on good terms, but if you didn't explain so she could understand it as other than an excuse, you were in trouble.

Practice things that promote Longevity.

There was no liquor or stuff like that in our family. There was no smoking, none of that, because my father said, "You learn to do those things that you will be alive to do later on and if you don't need it at the table when you sit to eat, then you don't need it." You ever see anybody around here swallowing a cigarette? You don't need it. . . . I had good genes, but I added to that by learning to live healthy, I never smoked, I never drank. I worked hard, educated myself and took care of my child. I've lived longer because I chose a healthy lifestyle that promoted longevity.

The right relationship will help you achieve your goals.

Yes, I feel that a woman should have a husband or boyfriend in her life. Think of a market basket, most of the time a market basket has two wide hooks. If you take the market basket and fill it, then take hold of the two wide hooks, and tried to carry it by yourself something is going to fall out. It's hard to manage by yourself. But if you took the same market basket, then fill it with something and you took one side your friend or your husband took the other side the two of you could go on down the road. If you try to handle both sides by yourself what's happening to the basket. Something is falling out; maybe the load is too heavy to carry alone. But with someone who is giving you the proper help you can carry the weight, keep it together and the two of you can go around the world with it. I really feel that a woman and a man should be together, and the longer you can stay in any relationship that is conducive to your getting along and getting ahead, the better.

You have to work toward future success today.

First, life is so short. You ought to make the best of it as possible. And there is nobody who has come back to tell me that it's better over there on the other side than it is over here. So you have to live now. You can't put things off. You have to work and make your goals and not live life talking about, "One day, I'm gonna." I do believe that.

Your problems are not unique.

When you have problems, you are not the only one. Everybody has problems and your problems aren't new.

There is nothing new under the sun, just a different way it was put together. You can't have a problem that somebody else hasn't already had one like it.

Is there a reason behind your romance?

Some of the things we identify with love have nothing to do with love. Girls have to also ask themselves questions about who they are involved with. Does he love me because of what I give him? Does he love me because of how I look? Does he love me because I have materialistic things? Maybe he loves you because you have a car and he needs a ride? You have to ask yourself, why does he want to be with me? Is it love or lust, or a temporary fix to some problem or need? There are a lot of people who think they love someone because another person meets a certain need. Be honest and identify your reasons for wanting to be with this person and why that person wants to be with you. Most of the time, if you're honest, you'll discover that what you were calling love is really not.

FAVORITE BOOK

The Miseducation of the Negro by Carter G. Woodson

Discussion

1 . **What is the difference between an excuse and an explanation?**

    A. Which would you prefer to hear?

    B. Are excuses good or bad?

    C. What are some common excuses that you hear often?

    D. When do you usually need an excuse?

    E. How can you avoid the need for an excuse?

2 . **Why would anyone want longevity?**

    A. Make a list of things that do not promote longevity

    B. Make a list of things that promoted longevity.

    C. How can you eliminate those things from your life that do not promote longevity?

3 . **What does a healthy relationship look like to you?**

    A. What elements are present in a healthy relationship?

    B. What are some of the characteristics of an unhealthy relationship?

    C. How can you quickly learn the difference?

4 . **Why is it important to work toward your goals today?**

    A. How long is appropriate to wait before going to work on your goal?

    B. What does postponing working on your goals usually produce?

    C. What can happen if you wait?

5 . **Make a list of your personal problems.**

    A. Are any of the problems on your list unique or mutually exclusive to you?

    B. How many people do you think have had the same problem?

    C. How did others solve those problems?

    D. What can you learn from the solutions of other people?

6 . **What are the underlying reasons for why you choose the person you are/were in relationship with?**

    A. Why do you thing that person chose you?

B.   Are they healthy reasons?

C.   Would you want your daughter to chose or be chosen for those reasons?

7 .   **What did you learn from Gertrude?**

A.   What did you like about her?

B.   What didn't you like?

C.   Was there anything you didn't understand?

D.   Is there anything you'd ask her for clarification or concerning a topic not covered in the interview?

E.   Are there any points that you disagree with her on?

Write a message to Gertrude in 100 words or less.

Knowledge can be communicated but not wisdom. One can find wisdom ... but one cannot communicate and teach it.

- Hermann Hesse

Dolola Louis Bates
The Entrepreneur

I have known Mrs. Bates for over twenty years. I met her when a friend called and told me he was in the hospital and his mother was coming and needed a ride from the airport. I picked her up and invited her to stay with me while she was in town. During this time my friend was in the hospital, his mom and I became unlikely friends. I liked her because she was very lively and comedienne funny. Over the years, we have visited each other often, we talk on the phone all the time, our families and friends have become united into one big happy family. I adopted her and everyone knows her as my Godmother. They assume that I've known her from birth, but I chose her to be my Godmother because she has so much wisdom and is a naturally caring person. She is never condescending or judgmental and never forgets to tell me how proud she is of me.

She has a way of phrasing things, and encapsulating them in a way that has stopped many a "pity party" in seconds flats. Over the years, she has given me so much guidance and I am very grateful. I laugh at her sayings. For instance, I was complaining about someone who told a lie that was a very obvious lie, and I was disturbed by it. I was very upset and going on and on about it, wondering why some people would not tell the truth. She said, "Baby, you can make your mouth say anything." It caught me by surprise, and I thought about it and it opened another world for me. From that point, I began to look at the difference between a person's actions, as opposed to the words spoken from their mouths. I have grown in wisdom and grace as a result of her influence in my life.

I was surprised when she wasn't enthusiastic about the interview process. She thought it was a great idea, but thought I should interview famous people or very successful ladies. But she had provided so much wisdom in my life that I was not going to accept "NO" for an answer. I had to nag her to do the interview. She said she prefers one-on-one spontaneous conversations, rather than being put on the spot. She finally agreed and sat down for the interview. It was great and we laughed our way through it. I found nugget after nugget of wisdom that I'm sure will inspire you. Even though the interview is shorter than what I would have liked, it is still packed with the kind of wisdom that can change lives and spare those who listen from heartbreak and mayhem. I invite you to examine the pages of her interview and decipher the rich lessons therein.

Dolola Bates

Dolola Bates

Dolola. . .

Janice: State your name, and date of birth for the camera.

My name is Dolola Louis Bates. My birthday is October 24, 1922. My mother's name was Joanna Louis and my father's name was Benjamin. I'm the last of 11 children. My mother had two sets of twins - her oldest boys and her youngest boys. There were seven boys and four girls in my family, me being the youngest. My mother died when I was six years old. She died in February and my father remarried in December. I had a beautiful step mother and beautiful family all together. We were a loving family. My step mother was just like a mother. She reared us to the best of her knowledge. My oldest brothers are about 15 years older than I am. My oldest sister had to take my mother's place between the months of February and December until my father remarried.

I went to school when I was 6 years old. I finished grade school and high school. I finished school in 1940. One of my sisters lived in Chicago, Illinois. And I came to live with her. And then I got married in 1942 - his name was Robert Wilson and he died young. Then I married again in 1954 to Mr. Clyde Bates. And to that union was one son. He was born in 1960. I was 39 years old. I got one grandchild who lives in Houston, Texas with his mother. Mr. Bates owned a cleaners from 1955 until his death in 1980. There you know it all. End of Interview (laughter).

Janice: What was your life like?

It was beautiful, I had a beautiful marriage. My husband was a very nice man. He was raised almost like an orphan, because his mother gave him away when he was six weeks old. And he told me when I first married him that he didn't have a mother. So when I met his uncle in Gary, Indiana, and he told me that she had given him away. It wasn't so much that she gave them away that I learned later in life that she was only 13 years old when she had him. And her uncle took him. Our life was beautiful, and I'm not just saying that. You can ask all of my friends and relatives. We had this one son, rotten, but he's mine. I love him and he loves me in his own way. He wrote me one of the nicest letters telling me how I bought him through a lot of trials and tribulations.

Janice: What was it like growing up?

It was beautiful. I was the baby. They said I'm spoiled, but I'm not spoiled. My older sister, that I came to Chicago to live with, her name was Naomi Flynn. My other sister was named Modine Gillerson, she lived in Little Rock, Arkansas. And she lived to be 93 years old, she just died on October the 14th. She died about four days before her birthday, October 19th, but we buried her on the 18th. But we always talked. We couldn't run around like the rest of the children, we had to be at home studying or doing whatever was necessary, because that was how our parents had raised us. My sisters and my brothers, all of them raised me. They say that they didn't do such a good job, but I think they did an excellent job.

Janice: What was it like being in business in the fifties and the sixties? When did you start the business?

In 1955. It was beautiful. We were in the cleaning business, dry cleaning business. When the polyester came in, it took an awful toll on us because that you could wash and wear. And it took a toll on our business. And then, it's just like I had a brother in Little Rock, Arkansas. He had a Barber College after the G.I.'s came back. And he always said that the Afro put him out of business because they weren't cutting hair. We worked hard. I was late twice in all the years we were in the business. The big '67 snowstorm, and one morning I got up and I had a flat. I opened at 7 and I closed at 7. I opened and you could say that I'm going to take my clothes by the cleaners on the way to work. You could also say that if you were two steps away from the door at 7 in the evening, you could go on back home. Because that's the way we ran our business. Because I think business should be run in a business way. My husband was one of the greatest pressers in the United States.

Janice: Who came up with the idea of starting a cleaning business? Did you work in one before?

My husband, that's what he was taught. He had a man that was in Mississippi, and this particular fellow gave him a job picking up things around the cleaners, when he was a child. And then he taught him how to press. That's where he got his experience. He came up with the idea. I was working for this manufacturer *Harshef and Martin;* they make men's clothes. And he says, since I know the cleaning business and you know how to sew – so that's how we got into the cleaning business. A friend of ours husband died; she had the business and we bought it from her. Her name was Ms. Mildred Jackson. We bought the cleaners from her in 1955 and we kept it until my husband died in 1980.

Janice: Out of all the items invented since you were born, what do you consider to be the greatest technological invention of your life time?

Well my father was very ahead of his time. He enjoyed life. When he'd get a newspaper, he'd read it cover to cover. I would have loved for my father to have seen a television. But he died in 1942, and they came out a little later. But now, I kinda go for that microwave. I think that microwave is something, I do.

Janice: Is there anything that you wish had never been invented?

Babies!! (laughter)

Janice: What is your life's greatest joy?

My baby boy! My greatest joy is my baby boy. He is 6 foot 4.

Janice: And your life's greatest sorrow?

Well, really, when I lost my husband - because we really had a good life.

Janice: When you look back over your life, do you have any regrets?

I am an honest person, and I do unto others as I have others do unto me. I try not to talk about anyone. Anything I have against you, I'm going to tell you.

Janice: How has the position and value of women changed over your lifetime?

Well we're a little more independent. A little more educated. In the olden days the woman had to go with what the man said. But now, we have women in high places, good places. And women have choices - if they want to stay home and can afford it, they can do that. If they want to be in the big time in corporations they can do that too. Women in my day didn't have those choices - most didn't in the 1920's and '30's.

Janice: What place do you think that she should hold?

As high as she can go. Anywhere she wants to be, wherever her mind and determination take her. She is no longer tied to a stove. I want one to be a president of the United States, is that the highest honor you can get? That's what I want a woman to be. You're smart enough to be president.

Janice: Thanks, but no thanks. You don't think that a woman should stay at home and keep the family and take care of the children?

Well that's a part of a woman's life. But in this day and time, with all these wants and these technological things, I think she should have help from her husband. They should share the parenting, cooking, cleaning. If she works and he works, they need to divide the responsibilities.

Janice: Do you think it was easier to be a girl when you were a girl, or do you think it's   easier for girls to be girls today?

I think it was easier in my time. Now there is so much distraction. Girls would like to be girls, but they really can't be girls, because they grow up too fast. You know the pedophiles and all these things, it's just hard to be a girl.

Janice: What is love?

What's love got to do with it? (laughter) I don't know really what love is, it's a feeling between two people. You know just like you got different kind of love. You've got romantic love with a man, you've got sister and brotherly love, you've got mother and father love. I can't define it. It is something that we all look for. There are a lot of things, confused or taken as love, that's not. Most of the time, it's lust or fear of being alone. Some women say, "I love him" when the truth is, I don't love him and I don't like him, but I don't want to be alone.

Janice: Do you think it's important for a woman to have a husband or a boyfriend in her life?

Yes, because it's more fulfilling.   Man was made for woman, and woman was made for man. God took out one of his ribs and made woman. So I really think that a woman should have a man and man should have a woman. But not just any man, a real one.

Janice: Do you think it is more important to have a man in her life, or fulfill her goals?

She can fulfill her goals with a real man.

Janice: What's the difference between a man, and a real man?

Well there are some men out there, and then there are others who just wear pants and happen to have a penis. Well there are some real men out there who support their woman and take care of their families. Then, there are other men who just wear paints and want to take from the family instead of support it. It's simple to tell the difference. If being with a man makes it harder for you to reach your goals and you find yourself always in a bad place, then you probably don't have a real man. If you are constantly sacrificing because you have to take up his slack, then maybe that's not a real man and it probably isn't love. It's more like co-dependency. If you're not with a real man, cut him loose or kick him to the curb, as they say.

Janice: What's an example of just the pants?

Somebody who doesn't think about anything - doesn't want to be anything and just want to get by. Like you have some of these ladies, they stay on welfare. And a man that will lay around there and take from a woman and her children. That is a pair of pants. A man who wants to be taken care of, who doesn't want to work, a man that will fight a woman. You know what I mean.

Janice: Yeah, my mother called them "breath in britches."

Janice: What one thing do you wish that women or young girls understood about life from your observation - that they just don't understand?

Well, that also comes from home training. You usually go with what you get in the home. There are so many babies out here having babies. They just need more home training. Life is not a game, it's something that you really have to live. I really can't pinpoint that because there is so much happening to young girls. I wish they understood that some decisions they make will be forever, like having babies, and not getting an education or some diseases are forever.

Janice: What do you wish they understood about love?

That love is something that you should take serious, not go from man to man. Just like anything else, it's supposed to be good for both people. Whatever you do, you're supposed to be true. If you're a ditch digger, be a true ditch digger. People can hurt you and make you get out of love. Love makes the world go round. We wouldn't have nothing. There wouldn't be one person if you didn't have love. That's what makes the world go round. You get together you love, and you make you some babies. That's love. That's the way I define it.

Janice: What one thing do you wish girls understood about longevity? You've made it to 80 years old and you've learned some things along the way.

Nice clean living, nice clean living. I have never drank, I've never smoked, I've never laid around with different men. I had a husband and I had a baby. And they should learn that right away, to take good care of themselves.   Live a nice, Christian life. I'm not just all religious.   Religion won't get you there unless you got something else. You have to have a person relationship.   Many preachers are just for money, some just for outside show.

Janice: So you've given us your recipe for longevity, what do you think it takes to make life fulfilling?

All the things we've talked about. Happiness. You know you can go a long way if you're happy. And happiness comes from love. Love is just about the main thing. Love makes the world go round.

Janice: I want you to think back and tell me what is the best advice anybody ever gave you?

My father, he always told us, this is the truth, that we were good as anybody but not better than nobody. I think that's the greatest advice that I've ever had.

Janice: As you look back over your life, is there one thing that you know now at 80 that you wish you had known at say 65 or 50 or 40?

No.

Janice: This is a question I'd like for you to imagine for a minute. Imagine that you had a 14 year old daughter, and for whatever reason you had to leave her. And she'd going to be alone there is nobody that you have to leave her with. And the advice that you give her now, is going to be the advice that

makes her be able to carry on or not be able to carry on. What would tell her? What advice would you give her?

Well I would have given her that advice all along. I would have instilled in her, how to treat her fellow man, how to do things like some mothers of today don't teach their children. I would have taught her how to cook and clean up, that's a part of living. I would just tell her to continue the way that I have taught her. Be nice to every one, and in return they will be nice to you. I'd tell her what my father told me.

Janice: We haven't heard on the camera the things that you have taught her over the years.

Okay, I've taught her cleanliness is Godliness. I've taught her that you've got to go to school and get you an education so that you can better yourself in life. And that's the main thing. Get you an education because you're going to need it. I don't care who you marry, you need your own to be self sufficient. Because you could marry a millionaire but he may not want you in the next 10 years or 5 years, so you have to be self-supportive you got school get your education and then you don't have to be reliant on him, you do it together as a couple.

Janice: What is the best way to raise children?

What the Bible says – "Don't spare the rod." All this psychology and all this stuff about time out, if you tell them to do something, they ought to do it. I think I'm pretty good after 80, I don't mistreat nobody. If you spare the rod, then you've lost the child. All children aren't alike. Some children are afraid of whippings and things, and you can tell them but most of them it don't hurt every once in a while to give them a spanking. I don't say abuse them. It's difference from abuse and spanking.

Janice: How do you motivate yourself?

I love to make other people happy. In return I get it back.

Janice: Tell me about your spiritual or religious beliefs?

Well I was born into the Baptist Faith, from my parents. I believe there is a Supreme Maker, but I got some questions about this modern religion and the old one too. Now God just don't come down here and do it for you. You can pray forever. Prayer, they say, changes things. But there is just some things I don't believe, but I know it is a Supreme Being. I believe that, I've been taught that all my life, and I can't deny that fact. But just some things in religion I don't like. First place, why have we got so many different faiths? One God. Jehovah Witness, they don't believe in this; Baptist don't believe in this, Catholics don't believe in this. We've got to come together, I believe we all will.

Janice: What do you see as a solution to the problems that young people are facing?

Drugs are messing our children up. And it's not done by the street dealers, it's done by rich folks with planes to fly the stuff over here. Rich folks on Wall Street, bringing drugs to my street. See I'm rapping! Drugs are ruining our young people.

Janice: What vision do you have for the future?

That I live to be another 80 years and feel as good as I do!

Janice: Tell me a little about what your daily routine is like.

I just had a discussion about that with somebody this morning. I always went to bed on time. We got a program called Wheel of Fortune. It comes on at 6:30. I love Wheel of Fortune. Very seldom do I stay woke long enough to see who wins. I have to call my girlfriend and ask who won. But I get up real early. Somebody told me this morning I'm not rested, but I think I am. I get a good 8 hours sleep - from 6 to 5 o'clock - I know I get 8 hours. I may get up once or twice and go to the bathroom because I'm taking water pills. I get up and do my work early in the morning.

Janice: What do you think about popular culture like music, clothes?

I pray that we get help - every day for these young people. These young men with their pants down, and young girls with dresses up to their navels. Dresses is too short. It's okay if you got pretty legs, flaunt them. But they are just too short. And the boys' pants are too low. I think they should have a dress code. The best thing they've done in public schools here is when they put all girls and boys in uniforms. So if one child has more than the other one, they don't feel bad, they all got on white blouses. white shirt, navy blue pants and navy blue shirt. I don't like the dress code that they are wearing out in the street. And this rap music, I don't like it, because it is so detrimental to the young people, because they are doing all that swearing and stuff and I think that you should be able to get your point across without that swearing. And music I love. I love every kind of music, but I don't go for that rap.

Janice: Weren't you the same woman I heard singing "Who let the dogs out," the other day? (laughter)

We was lettin' the dogs out, we wasn't cussin - we was just lettin' the dogs out. I said I like all kind of music, I don't like that vulgarism in there. But, sometimes you have to let the dogs out. Know what I mean?

Janice: So some rap you can go with?

I can go with it, I like music. I like Bach, I like Beethoven. I got a nephew that plays it. He's a genius. He plays concerts all over the world. The boy is good on music. But his elevator don't go all the way to the top. The elevator goes all the way to the top, but he gets off somewhere along the way, or the door doesn't open - something happens.

Janice: This is another one of those imagine questions. I want you to imagine that there was a lottery in the United States where they were going to take 1 senior citizen to the White House and talk to all of our political leaders and you won the lottery and got the chance to go to the White House and talk to our political leaders, representatives of Congress, President, etc. What would you talk about?

Well my concern is that they've got every other working place that have to retire at 65. Now why can't congress retire at 65? We've got one up there 99 years old. I don't care how brilliant he was when he went in there. I'm 80; he's got 19 years on me. I know his mind is not as sharp as it used to be. I can give you a lot of things that used to happen. But all this modern technology; but this man does not know we're paying him all that money. Retire all those old farts and let some young men and women come in and bring new ideas. The old women that's been there for years are interested in keeping their jobs, getting richer, holding my people down and keeping things like they were in slavery. I would tell them to get out like everybody else. Now that's what I'd tell 'em in Congress. I hope I win the lottery so I can go there. I'd tell them that there is just so much discrimination. It's just like my race, I'm an Afro-American, been one for 80 years. They do not treat us right. Now I'm going to get deep. They may not let us come to Washington. I think that 9-11 thing really woke them up. The United States has been bad to other countries. There is no way in the world I can love you and you have destroyed my country - Germany, Japan. And they are always over there in other people's business. I think the Lord brought us 9-11 to wake us up. Now we know how others fell when we bombed their countries. I would tell them all of that, I would speak my peace. I'm not too pleased with the way they treat my people. They bring every other nationality in here, they can get money. We've been slaving since the beginning of time. They've give money and a green card and reparations to the Japanese. And we've been here working hard since they brought us over here in chains from Africa. And I'm not that prejudice, I just want people to do unto others as they have others do unto them. You want me to tell them something else?

Janice: What about Medicare and the plight of the elderly?

It needs to be redone, just like Social Security. Medicare and all that needs to be redone for the elderly. Because, I have worked hard all of my life and the little Social Security that I do get is not enough to live on. We need more money to live good.

Janice: Here are some questions from some of the girls that I've worked with. One of the questions is, "What should you do when your mother does not act like a mother and she doesn't protect you?"

Well that's kind of hard. You've got to get someone that you can trust. There are always some good people out there. I know a case now, where this little girl doesn't trust her mother . . . this little girl, her mother had gotten a boyfriend, and he was staying at the house. And every time he'd get a chance he was trying to molest the little girl, and she told her mother. This is not a mother, this is a woman. She protected her boyfriend and she didn't protect the girl. And one day she was going to work, and she had to catch public transportation and it was right in front of the house. She realized she didn't have her badge to get into the factory and she came back in the house and the girl was screaming and hollering for help. And she didn't believe what the girl had been telling her all the time, which is a very sad mother. Both of them should be put in a hole underneath the jail.

Janice: What do you think the child should do?

At that age you probably wouldn't know how to go to the authorities, you know, like the policeman and things. But she would need to get somebody that she could talk to, an Aunt or a sister or somebody. Tell the teacher, the preacher, the Sunday School teacher. There I go rapping again.

Janice: This comes from the same little girl, "How do you stay hopeful in a hopeless world?"

We talk about young people; a lot of young people know how to pray. They say prayer changes things, I believe it helps. I'm not a religious fanatic, but I do believe. As I go back to saying, she should find someone that she could talk to. That's a hard life. She really didn't have a mother, she had somebody that birthed her, because a mother has always got to listen to the children and protect them. A mother will die before she sees one of her children harmed. She didn't have a mother, she had someone who bought her into this world. And that is not the definition of a mother. A good mother is always there for her children.

Janice: Out of all the periods of history that you've lived in, what has been the most interesting?   Like you've lived through the railroad era, the migration from people to the farm to the city, Civil rights, this current era. Out of all the periods that you've lived in, what is the most interesting to you?

I think when Martin Luther King was our leader and he was trying to get more rights for us, I think the Martin Luther King era, the civil rights ear. I believe that was the most interesting. We all had hope. We all were dreaming right along with Dr. King.

Janice: Is there anything you wish you'd done differently in your life?

I've had a beautiful life. I don't mean it's perfect - nothing is perfect. But I had good parents, even with a stepmother. I had a good husband, a provider and a good man.

Janice: At what age did you fall in love and how did you know it was love?

Ahhh shoot, that was the best thing in the world. I don't even know. I had puppy love at least 12 or 14. I was in high school. And the little boy, I could remember his name just like it was yesterday, he got me gum and got me candy and gave me a piece of it. I thought it was love.

Janice: At what age did you know it was true love?

I still don't know that. Infatuation maybe.

Janice: Do you feel you had a chance to finish all of your life's goals?

Yea, I'm through with that; I finished them. I'm just going to stay here another eighty years and worry you to death.

Janice: Do you have any other goals?

I want to go to Hawaii, I want to go to Hawaii, If I have to get out on the street and sell peanuts I'm going to Hawaii, but I hope it don't come to that. My son said he would help me go to Hawaii.

Janice: What is the biggest mistake you think young women make in love?

Being too much in love. Love is supposed to be a mutual thing. If you find out someone isn't doing what they are supposed to do for you, you get out of love. Love is just a word when it comes to that case. Don't let anyone mistreat you. I've never been abused. I've never been hit, because I tell all my lovers, "If my father and my mother didn't raise me, you can't raise me. So you better not hit on me 'cause if you do, there's going to be TROUBLE."

Janice: What advice would you give teenagers on relationships?

I don't know. That's a hard question. Just be careful of who you get in the relationship with because it can make a big difference in how your life turns out.

Janice: Why do you think teenagers do not listen to their parents?

Because they are teenagers. As they get older, some of them will listen and some of them won't. They are beginning to separate and get their own minds.

Janice: How has getting older changed your view points?

I've had a good outlook on life all my life. I love to live, love and be happy.

Janice: How do you cope with the loss of a loved one - the loss of a romantic love and the loss of one who is deceased?

My husband was sick and that was my love and I lost him. But I know every human being has got to go. I've done all I could; I had to run the cleaners to make ends meet because we wasn't old enough to get social security. And the little money we had would soon go away in sickness. He was sick 4 ½ years and when I lost him, I asked the Lord, I said, "Lord he suffered so bad, I'm not going to ask you to kill my husband, but I ask that your will be done." And it was done in the next two weeks. I just lost my sister, my oldest sister that partially raised me; that was my love, my sister. Every man born must die. I'm going to die, after I get another 80.

Janice: How do eliminate stress in your life?

Well, I get busy. When you see me real busy doing things, things may not be well. I handle sickness the same way. I just don't think you should just sit and die. Just get on with the problem at hand.

Janice: How do you instill in young girls to love themselves, so they don't look for someone else to feel that self-love for them?

Just teach them the right way how to take care of yourself, go to school. Do something for yourself. That is what everybody should do. You don't wait on another person to take care of you, you take care of yourself.

**Janice: As a black woman, how have you dealt with racism
in this country?**

That's kind of hard. I usually treat everybody like I want to
be treated. I've never been destitute. I don't have to deal
with the people too much. If you go to the store, you're
going to find everybody is different; you're going to find
some people that are nice, some that's nasty. I can deal with
it. If you don't want to talk to me, you don't talk to me. I
think the place that is most racist in our court rooms.

Janice: Why do you think parents have favorite children?

I don't know. Me being a parent to only have one, I've never
had to.

**Janice: How do parents instill the morals and values in their
children that they were reared with?**

That's hard to do because of the day. Children will tell you,
you're old fashioned. You know what I mean. The old-
fashioned thing got us by. But a lot of these modern things
won't get them by.

**Janice: The last question, is there anything that you thought
that I would have sense enough to ask you, that I didn't ask
you?**

Now you know how I feel about you. I think you are one of
the most intelligent young women that I know. And I tell
them all. You are a beautiful person.

Lessons from Dolola

Know the difference between a good man and a bad one.

Well there are some real men out there who support their woman and take care of their families.

Then, there are other men, who just wear pants and want to take from the family instead of support it. It's simple to tell the difference. If being with a man makes it harder for you to reach your goals and you find yourself always in a bad place, then you probably don't have a real man. If you are constantly sacrificing because you have to take up his slack, then maybe that's not a real man and it probably isn't love. It's more like co-dependency. If you're not with a real man, cut him loose or kick him to the curb, as they say.

The Wrong Relationship can ruin your life.

Just be careful of who you get in a relationship with because it can make a big difference in how your life turns out.

Learn to provide for yourself.

Just teach them the right way how to take care of themselves. Make sure they go to school so that they will have options. Do something for yourself that will create a good future for yourself. That is what everybody should do. Don't wait on another person to take care of you, take care of yourself and never lose sight of your goals. Provide for yourself and don't have any children until you can afford to properly provide for them.

Report all forms of abuse.

Things like this[molestation] happen, but if your mother doesn't believe you or help you, keep telling people, tell anyone that will listen until you find someone willing to help you. Don't stop telling and don't give up just because your mother doesn't believe you. And don't be embarrassed, because you're not a bad person. The abuser is the bad person, the criminal and if you don't keep telling, he'll get away with it and do the same thing to someone else. Call the authorities. Depending on how old the child is she probably wouldn't know how to go to the authorities. Look up the number to the police station, or better yet call information (411) and get the number for the police station and tell the police. Then try to find somebody that you could talk to, an Aunt or sister or somebody to help you see, that you are not bad in any way.

Love comes and love goes.

Love is supposed to be a good thing. If you find out someone isn't doing what they are supposed to do for you, you get out of love. Love is just a word when it come to that case. Don't let anyone mistreat you. I've never been abused. I've never been hit, because I tell all my lovers, "If my father and my mother didn't raise me, you can't. So you better not hit me, because if you do there is going to be TROUBLE."

Discussion

1. **List some men that you consider to be "real men."**

   A. What about their actions make you consider them to be "real men?"

   B. Do these men have some characteristics in common?

   C. Is there anyway you can pick them out of a crowd without prior knowledge of them?

   D. How do they differ from men you don't consider to be real men?

   E. What are the characteristics of a man, who is not a real man?

   F. How would you be able to identify him without prior knowledge?

2. **How could the wrong relationship ruin your life?**

   A. What consequences could be associated with a wrong relationship?

   B. Are any of the consequences you mentioned permanent?

C. What signs could you watch for that would indicate you're about to enter a potentially dangerous relationship?

D. Formulate a list of questions that you could ask yourself that will help you decide if a relationship is good or not.

3. **How can education provide options for you?**

A. What are your career options without a high school diploma?

B. What are your career options with a high school diploma?

C. What are your career options with a college degree?

D. What are your career options with a graduate degree?

E. What does an education open?

F. What doors are closed without an education?

4. **What should you do if you are being abused or know someone who is**

A. How should you tell?

B. Who is required by law to help you?

C. Who could you talk to for support?

D. What agencies handle abuse complaints?

5 . Is love a permanent thing?

     A. How long do you usually stay in love?

     B. How long do love relationships normally last?

     C. Is it possible to fall out of love?

     D. What are the reasons to fall out of love?

     E. Do the parties always fall in or of love at the same time?

     F. What happens if you fall out of love with someone who still loves you?

     G. What do you do if you still love someone who no longer loves you?

6 . What did you learn from Dolola?

     A. What did you like about her?

     B. What didn't you like about her?

     C. Was there anything that you didn't understand in the interview

     D. Is there anything that you'd ask her to clarify or to comment on that was not covered in the interview?

     E. Are there points that you disagree with her on?

Write a message to Dolola in 100 words or less.

The real voyage of discovery consists not in seeking new landscapes, but in having new eyes.

- Marcel Proust

Jodale Brodnax
The Paranormal Enthusiast

I met Jodale for the very first time when a group of women I know decided to have High Tea at the Ritz Carlton hotel. She was wearing a beautiful Christmas vest with bells on it and she didn't rest until she went from table to table making the acquaintance of everyone present. I could see that she could easily be the life of the party.

Later, we formed a study group and Jodale was a member of the group. Getting to know Jodale was a classic example of why you should never judge a book by its cover. My first impression was that she was a little "dingy." She was blond, extremely bubbly and always smiling. Some of the blond stereotypes came to mind, but boy, was I wrong. I misjudged her. I have learned some very exciting lessons from Jodale. If you sit and listen to her for more than five minutes, you will be amazed. She always has a fresh perspective that others in our group seemed to miss. Most of us were pseudo professionals, trained to be logical and rational, so much so that we often missed the simplicity in some of the material that we studied. Jodale, however, didn't miss anything. She is bright, articulate and open-minded. She has a way of taking the complex and making it simple for those of us who tend to make things more complicated than it needs to be. In the two or more years that we shared in the study group, we became friends and she was high on my list to interview, because I really respected her passion, intelligence and dedication to learning. She is loving and sensitive and is extremely supportive. She always manages to surprise you with her wisdom.

Jodale Brodnax

Jodale. . .

Janice: I want you to give me a brief overview of your life. The things that if anyone were writing your life story, it would be important for them to know - like where you came from, where you were born, how many siblings you had.

I was born on August 13, 1931 In Dallas, Texas. My dad was a traveling salesman. My older sister was born in Chicago. My younger sister was born in Ohio and we lived in Dallas until I was three and we moved to Chicago until I was eight, and then we moved to Atlanta. And I've been here ever since.

I went to Durham grammar school and high school in the Atlanta area. And I still meet with five of my friends; we call each other first grade friends. I actually came in the third grade. All of my life I have loved football. Friends of my dad took us to all to the Georgia State football games when I was growing up. And I just fell in love with the game of football, which may sound crazy for a girl, but I loved it. I loved to watch it. And I even had my own little football outfit, when I was about 12 years old. I played with the boys in the neighborhood. There weren't any girls to play with, so I played with the boys. I was one of the boys. But I dreamed and visualized that some day I would be an All American at Georgia Tech. That's where I went to the football games. In high school I was a cheerleader for the football team and I loved that. I met my husband, George Brodnax, at age 17; he was the man of my dreams. He was born and raised in Atlanta, and we will have been married 52 years in December. We got married when I was 18. We raised four children, two boys and two girls, and I have 10 grandchildren.

I've been active in a lot of things all my life. I've always been interested in the paranormal because as a child I had many so-called psychic experiences of knowing things in advance and not knowing why and being told, don't ask. My mother was this way, so she was very understanding with my experiences because she had had some paranormal experiences. I learned to communicate with my mother when we were apart which was unique in a way. I learned that you don't talk about psychic things because people make fun of you or are afraid of you; so I was very careful.

When I got married I think my husband didn't like the thought that I had this gift. I think I put myself on a shelf so to speak, because of other people's fears. And the first 20 years of my marriage, I didn't read anything. My dad really didn't want me to get married at age 18. He said, "You're dropping out of school to get married and you won't get a college education and you won't be any smarter than you are now." So I didn't read a book for 20 years. I just concentrated on raising four great children.

They all went to college. I was very pleased. I have four college graduates. We have been a very loving, caring family. We did lost a grandson who committed suicide five years ago, which was very difficult. He was my oldest daughter's son. It happened on his sister's 18th birthday; he was 15. He shot and killed himself. We don't know why; he left no note. So we've had to deal with it. It's been the most traumatic thing in my life. To have something like that happen. We all, of course, loved him very dearly.

I am interested in so many things, and through the years, just about 30 years ago, I got into a course on parapsychology at Oglethorpe College with a psychic teacher and loved it. I found out that there were other people like me out there who hear things, see things, feel things and know things that other people don't seem to. I met Kim Lemon in the class, and we started meeting regularly to share our experiences. We knew that we couldn't talk about it with other people. But this one group was all very open, so we met every week for months to share our experiences

I just love life. I'm having a wonderful time. I'm an entrepreneur. My husband and I do many things. We travel a lot; we've been all around the world. I enjoy being with people. I love people. I'd rather go to a party where I didn't know everybody than to know everybody in the room. Because I find people fascinating, I love to listen to who they are, what they are, what they are about.

Janice: Aren't you a breast cancer survivor?

No I had lung and stomach cancer 10 years ago.

Janice: How did you survive?

Well I had nursed a dying mother for four years. She was in a nursing home. We had her back and forth between different nursing homes and personal care homes. She just wasn't happy any more. She had really lost her mind. It was up to me to care for her in that respect, to see that she was happy and healthy. So for four years I went through an awful lot of stress. Two weeks after she made her transition, I was diagnosed. First they thought it was viral pneumonia and it was clouding my lungs. So for next four months, every month I would go in for another X-ray and they would say, "You've got viral pneumonia." That started in January; in April they decided they saw something besides that. So they went in and they found that I had lymph node in my right lung and they removed half of the lower part of my right lung. And they told me they got it all, and I would be fine, I was one of the fortunate ones. And within days, I couldn't' quit hurting, the pain was increasing daily. Within a couple of weeks, I was back in the hospital, literally screaming in pain. And they found out I had cancer. The lining of my stomach was covered in ulcers, and they wanted to take part of my stomach, but I wouldn't let them. They wanted me to start Chemo right away. I refused that because I had taken two of my best friends to chemo sessions and watched them slowly die. And I just said no, and so for the next five months I touched every base I could touch with supplements. I did guided imagery, meditation, I taught classes on meditation and guided imagery and positive thinking and all that type of information. I had taught classes in my home.

I was very interested and very knowledgeable in that field. And I was a regular mediator. But the stress of my mother's illness weakened my immune system, and I've learned since that stress is the number one killer actually; it does weaken your immune system and you have trouble resisting illnesses. Where the cancer came from I don't know. They don't know what causes it for sure. Why it hit my lung, I don't know because I am not a smoker. I never smoked, but my husband did and my father did. And they said second-hand smoke can be as dangerous. So in April they found the cancer and removed a part of the lung. I said no chemo, so I had a friend who guided me with all these wonderful products. She said you do what I tell you to do, and I'll get you well. And she was an elderly woman and I trusted her and I did everything she told me to do. And gradually I was getting better. But in September of that year, in '91, my sister, who is a nurse, and one of daughter-in-laws is a nurse, they came to me and said the doctor said that I only have a couple of months to live. "You've got to have chemo." So I said, all right, but I'm going to limit it. So I had five shots, on the fifth shot, the needle slipped out of my arm and burned my arm and they had to pack me in ice for 24 hours. I said, "That's it, I'm out of here, no more Chemo." And so they went back into my stomach and I didn't have any cancer.

So luckily the combination of all the alternative things I was doing, plus the chemo - thankfully I had gotten stronger when I went on chemo, and had five months to build my system up. So I could handle it. Chemo is so destructive, it kills the cancer cells but it kills the system and everything else. So all the things I was taking really contributed to the reason I survived. And I had people praying for me and I did guided imagery every day - I had a tiger named Tony who went into my lung every day and ate the cancer. Just all those types of mental tricks you can do to convince your body of a certain thing. I had a strong desire to live; I was not ready to give up. I have a beautiful family. I was determined, I was going to beat it, and I didn't care what anybody said. My doctor, in the beginning, didn't think I was going to make it to six months. Lung cancer is very destructive. I was very fortunate. I worked at it and I think you have to touch every base if you are going to survive. So I used all the tools of the trade and I made it. It's been ten years November 23.

I walked every day when I was sick. I didn't care that I hurt when I walked. I played tapes, I had the walkman and I would listen to very upbeat and positive music, I would sing along with it. I loved Whitney Houston and I would listen to one of her songs every day, along with some of the "I am woman" kinds of songs, that are so motivating and encouraging. Of course I had days when I was very down. Every day I went upstairs and I painted. I painted t-shirts; I did over 400 shirts, purses, vests, scarves, gloves - you name it, I painted it. That's something that gave me something to look forward to every day. I couldn't wait to get upstairs and start my painting, and I did some beautiful things. I was getting good at it. And my family said, 'No more shirts, Mother, please." I gave them away and sold them at the bizarre and church and things like that.

That was a creative outlet for me. And I think that's important to have something to get your mind off of yourself. Find something you really enjoy doing that you can look forward to.

Janice: So what advice would you give someone who is fighting any kind of illness?

Be as "up" as you can be, which is challenging, you just have to work at it. You have to touch all bases; you have to do a lot of research on your own and reading and talking to others. I always suggest people learn to meditate; go within and pull from the source of strength that is within you. Use guided imagery and come up with something that you can pretend is working on your body - maybe little miniature doctors and nurses. Like I said, I had Tony the tiger. Get people to pray for you, I believe very strongly in the power of prayer. Try to keep a good attitude as possible. I was in a support group which was very helpful. I was in one group that was very negative; all they could talk about was their aches and pains, so I got out of that group and got into another group.   That was very uplifting and very encouraging; it was all about being creative and going within and using the God-given power within. .

Janice: Has there been one particular book or anything that has made a difference in your life?

A good friend introduced me to a book called *Key to Yourself* by Venice Bloodworth. It was only a dollar back then; I think it's now about nine dollars. The prices have gone up; they keep reissuing it with a new cover. But to me, it answered so many questions that I wanted answers to. And I remember for a long time I was buying it by the dozens, and giving them to everybody because I was so excited about it. This was a woman from Atlanta, she wrote about 75 years ago, but it was full of truths and it is still important today.

And there have been a lot of books, because thirty years ago, I discovered that I could start reading and going to classes and learning. I was reading books every few days, and over a period of seven years, I read close to 400 books, all of them motivation or spiritual books, anything to improve myself. I was so hungry because I had felt like I wasted 20 years, because I didn't do any studying and reading, and have found all these new things, education books, I just read every one of those. They just got me so excited. And other books about people that are intuitive. I'm still in study groups, now we are studying this new book, *Excuse Me Your Life is Waiting*, by Lynn Grabhorn.

Janice: What do you consider to be the best invention of your life time?

The best invention? I think the television. When I was a teenager, my dad was in appliances and we had one of the first television sets in the neighborhood. I would sit and watch it all the time. On the weekends they would televise high school games and everyone would come to our house and watch the games. Gradually throughout the years, with the children, I think television played a big role in all of our lives. I guess that to me would be the most interesting invention that I can think of.

Janice: Is there anything that was invented that you wished had not been invented?

Oh my goodness, sometimes the telephone!

Janice: What do you consider to be your life's greatest joy?

Children are special. Grandchildren are special. Friends are special. Family is special, and I'm so blessed to have so many wonderful friends. And I think to be able to think and create is a joy. When I was a child I was lucky. I won things all the time and I knew that whatever I wanted I could get. That may sound strange, but even as a child I knew, or maybe I didn't know, that it was a gift - that if you think about something and you really want it, think about it and you'll get it. And I usually did. I was Ms. Freshman, Ms. Sophomore, Ms. Senior, and Ms. Junior. I knew that I was going to win them, I just made up my mind that I was going to win.

Janice: And what do you consider your life's greatest sorrow?

Losing my grandson.

Janice: Is there anything that you wish you had done that you didn't do, that you regret?

I would love to have a college education. For a long time I felt real inferior to my friends because all my friends went on to graduate from college. But I fell in love at 17 and wanted to get married, so I dropped out of college and got married. My husband was already out of college, four years older. So girls think that's why they go to college to get a man, well I had a man so I didn't need to go to college. I had the guy that I wanted. Now, I'm going to Senior U, I've been going there for five years. These are all senior citizens who meet at Mercer College. We take different courses. We don't take tests; we're not graded or anything. But we have all different types of course we can take. And I've enjoyed that thoroughly. I'm an ongoing student.

Janice: How has the position of women and value of women changed over your   lifetime?

It's changed quite a bit. I remember years ago my grandmother and I used sit on the front porch. She told me that when she was younger, she could not vote. And that just upset me terribly, because I thought, why wouldn't they let her vote? And that just stuck with me for years. And when I turned 18, I registered the day I was 18, and I have not missed voting since. I'm trying to make up for my grandmother not being able to vote.

I think women today are much stronger and more assertive. Women are out there doing things. I mean when I got married, women just didn't work. Sometimes women worked as a secretary or something like that, but there weren't women executives. And there is that "glass ceiling" that still exists to some degree today. But I think the women are expected to work even though they have babies; they go back to work, which I don't agree with. I think they need to be home with the kids. But they seem to manage okay.

Janice: Do you think it's easier to be a girl now than it was when you were a girl?

No, I had a fun childhood because we traveled a lot in the summertime. I had two sisters, and a lot of good friends. We rode our bikes and went roller-skating we played "kick the can" at night. We never worried about locking doors, I could walk anywhere I wanted to go at night and never worry about it. Mother was never concerned about it. We just didn't have to worry about things. But now, if I keep my grandchildren, my daughter-in-law will say, "Don't let them out of your sight. If you take them to the mall you hang on to them." They are so afraid they are going to be snatched or something. So there is a lot of fear today. I think it's in the children because the parents make them fearful about it - somebody is going to snatch them or something. I know my daughter-in-law is petrified somebody is going to take one of her children. We didn't have to worry about that. I think the girls today have a lot of freedom.

Janice: Do you think it's important for a woman to have a husband or boyfriend in her life?

It was the most important thing in my life growing up. I wanted dates, and so that was part of my goal growing up. I couldn't wait to get married and have a baby. So that was what was important, to have a husband, to have a baby to have a family. But I don't want to judge the women today; it's a different time than it was when I was growing up. I remember one of my friend's mothers got a divorce, and it was just scandalous that her mother had gotten a divorce, and now I have three of my four children have gotten divorces and, of course, they are remarried happily, thankfully, But it was a scandal back 40-50 years ago - or you just didn't talk about it. And if somebody lived with somebody, nobody knew it.

Janice: What one thing do you wish that women understood today about life? Love? Longevity?

They must know that they must love themselves so that they can love others - the more you love yourself. It takes regularity; you must constantly love yourself and not put yourself down. The more you can love yourself, the happier you'll be and loving others will be easier. I think love is energy; it's a thought, it's a feeling. It's so important to love, love everything, and the more you can love, you'll feel better. It's important to be loved and feel loved. We didn't used to do that, but now you just talk to somebody and in ten minutes it's. "Hey I love ya, love ya kid." I can remember 50 years ago when my husband's best friend came home from Korea - he'd been wounded, and we shook his hand, we didn't hug him. And today I met a lady for the first time and I hugged her when I met her. Love, or the importance of touch, is so much more a part of our psyche today. He had almost died in a war and we shook his hand when he came home. And today we would have just hugged and hugged and told him we loved him. And I'm not embarrassed to tell people I love them, and I would hear it a lot more. My husband and I tell each other two or three times a day how much we love each other. We didn't use to do it, but we do it now.

Janice: What do you think girls should understand about life?

That they are special. Everybody is special and that you are connected to source. You cannot be separated from the energy of God; you're like a fish in the ocean, you're in it, you breathe it, you drink, you can't be separated from it. You are a part of it wherever you are. I think more people need to go within and find it within themselves instead of looking out there for it. I grew up being told in a Christian church that you need to find God inside yourself. I just wish that more people were taught that being still and knowing that God dwells within them and is always there for them. Everyone can go to this source, this energy, this unconditional love. One thing I learned from A Course in Miracles that I studied over a period of three years, is the importance of affirmations. I repeated an affirmation such as "Jodale, I unconditionally love and support you just the way you are." It just made me feel good. You say God and I are one; there is an oneness in everything. You can't separate yourself. I wish Christianity would teach what was originally taught but they've gotten away from it; they've incorporated all this fear and sin bit - I'm no good, and you're no good and all of the judgmental stuff. And yet Jesus taught nothing but love, forgiveness and non judgment. It's there in the Christian teaching, but now they come up with this negative stuff. It just sets me off (laughter). I want to say, no, no, no, don't fill them with all that fear - don't make them feel guilty. Religions are built on guilt. You don't do this, you don't do that, or you're going to burn in hell - the devil is gonna get you. I told my son-in-law I don't believe in the devil. He said you better believe in him. I said, well you can have him I don't want him.

Janice: What do you think girls should understand bout longevity?

If you can accept the theory of reincarnation that you know before we come into life, how long we're planning on staying or what's the reason we come in, the purpose we've come in to learn. It's like you come in to college and you get out your catalog and you pick the school that has the courses that you want. And that's the same thing with life. You choose your parents, which I accept that was a revelation to me that I did pick my mom and dad, but I'm thankful I did - I got their good genes.

It brought me into where I wanted to be and what I need to experience and to learn. I chose that college to go to because it had the courses I wanted to progress in my life and when I learned what I wanted to learn, I will leave and maybe come back when I am ready to evolve my soul. It's an ongoing process – we come from God we go back to God. but we never left God, if you can grasp that. But it's evolving. I have no fear of dying because I know I will just transcend. I told my friend I believed in reincarnation, and she said. "Well you know you can't be Christian if you believe in that." And I said, "I guess I'm not a Christian." She said, "No, you're not, you cannot believe in that."   I said, "Why not," and she said, "Because it's not in the bible." I said, "Well it works for me and I'm happy with that theory. I really truly believe it. I know I've been here before. I know that God just wouldn't give me one opportunity." Why would a child come in with cerebral palsy and only live 10 years of live? That's not fair. That child came in for a reason, maybe to teach somebody compassion and love. But they volunteered. I think some of the most sick children, I think are very vital souls who come in to help people learn a lot and not judge and care for them and so I always look on people with deformities and real serious problems to be very special people.

Janice: **What do you consider to be your recipe for fulfilling life?**

Caring, being a caring person, caring about everybody. It's challenging sometimes, you may not approve of something that someone is doing, but you still have to love them - because that love, that spark of God is within them, even that man in the gutter, the drunk, still has that spark within him. And loving him could help him because it helps you. So learning to be more caring and not judging, and that's challenging too.

Janice: **What is the best advice that anyone has ever gave you?**

I've been given a lot of advice through the years and I've read so many things, and studied and shared and listened in on so many things. But, the best advice, I've gotten is to love yourself, because you can't love someone else unless you love yourself first. And that kind of made an impact on me because I thought I loved everybody already, but loving myself came first, and then I had more love to give. The more I could love me multiplied the love I had for others.

Janice: **Imagine now that you have a 14 year old daughter. And you are getting ready to leave her, and you want her to**

have some life lessons that will take her forward from this point. What do you want her to know?

That I care, that I will always care and that I will always be there for her regardless of what happens. She can feel free to come to me with anything, any problem, any challenge, any question that she may have about anything, and I will listen to her, care for her, and look after her, if that's what she wants. And I would hope that she would learn to love herself and not be fearful and know that there is help available when you ask. Like Jesus said, "Ask and you shall receive." I would encourage her to not be afraid to ask, to seek, to knock and be able to ask people for help - know that God is always with you and the energy of the guardian angels or whatever. There is always help available. And I would also encourage her to take time to be still and incorporate time for meditation everyday. Be still and go within and find that source. I used to say that meditating was the bottom line and it's what brought everything together. You could think and be positive and affirm things, but when you took it within in the quiet of your mind. it is like cementing everything together. My son, when he was in college said, "Mom, I just never have any time to do anything." And I said, "Pete, if you would take time to meditate, you would have more time." He had trouble grasping that. But when he began to meditate, he realized that if he took time to be still, to contemplate what he needed, he managed to fit everything in.

Janice: What do you think is the best way to raise children?

Be there for them, to love them and care and listen to them.
Oh! Listen, listen, listen and praise them and be a part of
what they are part of. If they are in sports go to their games.
We must have gone to a million games. Encourage them and
be there for them. Mother was always there for us. Even
though she was involved, she was almost always at home
when we got home from school - she made it a point. She
would be there, we would come into the kitchen and she'd be
in there baking something for dinner or a neighbor, and she
would listen to us and we would tell her about our day. And
that was an important part of my day, to be able to tell my
mother what went on in school that day. And I did the same
thing with my kids - I made the point to be there – "What
happened today?" "Who'd you play with?" "What'd you
do?" "What'd you learn? Know what they are doing, know
their friends, who they are with. You can give them freedom,
but you've got to have rules too, you've got to be disciplined.
And they've got to respect that. My kids would come home
and say, "Well Mary Ann is doing this or that; I would say
"Well that's fine at Mary Anne's house, but at our house we
don't do that." Her mother has rules; we have rules. We
don't do that. And they respected that. Children want
discipline; they want to know that you care and you support
them and listen to them.

**Janice: What should you do if your mother does not want to
be, nor does she act like a mother, and she never protects
you?**

Well, maybe there is a grandmother or a friend or teacher or someone at the church that you can talk to. I know as a little girl I often went to my grandmother's when they moved down from Ohio. I'd go to my grandmother's and sit and talk to her. So there are other people that you can go to. You can sit down and talk with her and tell her you'd like to spend time with her. If she rejects you, then know it's not you she's rejecting; she's rejecting herself, and she's missing the opportunity to be a part of your life. It's sad when a mother don't participate in a child's life. But if you can find a mentor, a friend, a neighbor, family member, then go and tell them you're lonely. Don't be afraid to ask for help. Go to your teachers.

Janice: How do you tend to stay hopeful in a hopeless world?

Well first of all I don't think this is a hopeless world. I think life is something that you have to work. I believe that people who give up, miss out on a lot of things and they create more problems. Look for the sunny side of the street or whatever, and keep your chin up. All those things sound corny but they really do mean something. But you can pull yourself up. And I've seen people who have pulled themselves up from really low pits, but it can be done.

Janice: Out of all the periods of history, what is your favorite period and why is it?

I think that every passage that you go through is a favorite when you are in that period. I'm in a great age now. I love being where I am, I really do. I am proud that I am still here. I am having fun, I am thankful that my husband is healthy and I'm happy. I have a lot of good friends and I love to go to parties and movies. I love to travel; we went to Alaska a couple of years ago.

My husband is 74 and he is slowing down some, but we play golf a couple of days a week. We go out with our friends to dinner. We had a Halloween party Saturday night and we had 18 people there, all in costume. We were all in our 70's and a couple of them in their 80s; we dressed up like kids and had a ball. We told ghost stories. And we don't have any worries really about money, to a degree, and what's going on the world. But basically we are having a good time. Getting 60, 70 and 80 years old does have its down side, because you often have a lot of different aches and pains, you know. I hear some of my friends complaining, but fortunately I don't have much of that. Overall, I think it's a good kind of life right now for me.

Janice: Do you feel as if you had a chance to finish all your life's goals?

I hope so! I'm counting on it. I've got one big goal that I am working on, and if I keep being positive about it, not giving up, then I feel I will have it happen. I feel I have accomplished a lot of things in my life. I've set goals for years. I've been treasure- mapping, I put pictures on a large piece of paper of things I want in my life. I've got most everything I've put on my map. It's beautiful that you can create your future with pictures and affirmations and things like that.

Janice: What is the biggest mistake you believe young women make in love?

I think these young girls that go out and have sex at 12 and 14 years old are literally destroying their lives. Sex can be beautiful with somebody that you truly love, and it's very meaningful. But these kids that are running around jumping in and out of bed with other people, it's just sad. It breaks my heart because many of them are getting all kinds of diseases. They have to live with those things all the rest of their lives. And if they have an abortion, they have to live with that for the rest of their lives. All those things that happen when you're young never go away; they are there in your mind. You can bring them back and just relive them even if it was fifty years ago; you still feel the emotions from that experience. I would hope that they would wait until they are really mentally prepared. I don't think that marriage is a necessity, of course I grew up thinking at that time that it was. That you didn't have sex unless you were married. It's a different world now, but I wish we could go back to that again. Because women are creating an awful lot of heartaches and problems down the road; they don't realize it, the pain and heartaches. Just wait until the time is right, financially, physically, mentally and emotionally mature enough to handle the situation.

Janice: Why do you think teenagers don't listen to their parents?

Because most of the time what parents have to say is negative. "Don't do this, don't do that." "You're too dumb!" "You're too stupid!" "Why should I let you do that?" "Why don't you grow up, you're such a baby?" I think the put-downs that some of the parents do to children is wrong. It's okay to discipline them, but listen to them and don't control or judge them. Find out what it is that you want them to do, if you can get them talking. But that has got to start young. You can't wait until they are 14 years old and say, "Okay, tell me about yourself." It's got to start with children - reading to them, listening to them, playing with them, being with them, and hugging and loving them. I told all four of my children to tell those children that you love them everyday, and that you're glad that you've got them, and you thank God that they're your children. I've emphasized that with my children - make sure they know you love them. A lot of children don't feel that love. They are not told they are loved, they are told that they are stupid. And if you tell somebody they are stupid long enough, they are going to believe it, and it hurts. I would encourage everybody to tell everybody they love them.

Janice: how has getting older changed your viewpoints on things?

I guess I'm more open. I'm more patient, hopefully. That's a challenge because I've always been very impatient with myself and others. I'm sure I've changed my viewpoints in many ways, the way I look on things. I used to be very judgmental and I'm not that way anymore. I work at not being judgmental - just accepting people for who they are. If they are doing the best that they can do, then that's okay. When I work with somebody I hope that I will get through to them and they'll listen. And if they don't, then okay, that's their choice. I've come to a point where I can say, that's their decision if they want to do that, just don't go hurt anybody.

Now that's when I go get upset. When I see somebody hurting somebody else or even gossiping; I just don't want to hear people talking about other people. I don't like being negative or putting someone down. I just don't want to be part of that.

Janice: If you had to do it all over again, what changes would you make and why?

I think I would have read more as a child. I wish I had studied a little bit better, been a little better student. although I was a B average student. I think I probably would have been a little nicer than I was.

I would like to have a college education. Not absolutely necessary, but it could have broadened my intellect a little more. I'd like to travel more, although we've been very fortunate and we've traveled a lot. I wish I had told more people I loved them. I wished I would have kept in contact with some of the people that I have lost contact with.

Janice: You say you fell in love at 17, how did you know for sure that that was love?

I had actually been going with another guy from out of town since I was 15. I was very much in love with the guy – I thought he was the one. He was a good looking football player; he was very sexy and he had gorgeous eyes. I thought he was God's gift to me and I was only 15 at the time. And I fell head over heels in love with him – I thought he was the one. In fact, I was going to go off to the University of South Carolina to be with him in January of '49. I had turned 17. A friend took me to a basketball game and I had seen this guy play football at Georgia Tech and we met at a basketball game and it was like "Goodbye Ed, Hello George." (laughter) He had just made All American; he was the big football star; tall, blond and good looking. I fell in love with who he was, what he was, his looks, and everything was just right on. He asked me for a date and we went out the next night and we knew immediately. I don't know what it was; it was like I've been looking for you all my life. And it was kind of crazy because I was literally packed to go off to college the next week. We were going to sneak and get married and everything. But when George came along, and the second date we had the next nigh, we were talking about getting married; we knew we were in love, we knew this was it.

Janice: Is there any age that you think a woman is ready for marriage?

Again, it depends upon the individual. Some women are ready to get married at 17 or 18, I was ready. It was my goal in life to be married and have children and find the best looking guy I could find, so I really fulfilled what I wanted at seventeen, and got married at 18.

I think getting an education is important, very important. Of course you can get it later too. If you can get it before you get married, all the better. Know what you want, set your goals, just don't rush out and get married to the first guy that comes along. Know him and know what he wants. Become a friend - be friends before you become lovers. And wait for the sex. Really know that this is the person for you. And you'll know the feeling that you don't want to be separated from them –

you hang on to everything that they say. You feel goose bumps when they touch you. You know that's the person that and you can't get them out of your mind. You want to touch them; you want to feel them.

Janice: This girl writes, "Should I tell my parents I am not a virgin and that I am currently sexually active?"

How well do you know your parents? (laughter) Will they hurt you? I would try to bring them both together with maybe a third party – a grandmother or good neighbor or friend or minister or somebody. You can have a joint meeting about your concerns. And say, "I think it's time I be honest with you." Maybe go talk to the minister first and see what he suggests and how to deal with it. Hopefully the child will not let that happen. They can communicate with the parents.

Janice: How do you cope with the loss of a love, and the loss of a lover?

When I was 12 years old I was madly in love with a little boy that was the son of some friends of my mom and dad. I thought he was the cutest thing that ever was. I thought he was so great and I introduced him to my girlfriend, and that was a mistake because they ended up getting married eventually. But that broke my heart. I know I cried for days when he told me he was dating my best friend. Losing a lover – I've never really lost a lover. The young man before I met George that I thought I was in love with, I was kind of glad to get rid of him because I found George, I had replaced him. I never really lost a lover. It would be difficult I'm sure, because I can remember even how I felt as a small child - that it hurt. By getting busy and going out and meeting other people; there are other fish in the sea. If you lose one, go get another one.

Janice: How do you eliminate or reduce stress in your life?

I meditate every day, that' part of my life, meditating. I know that relaxes me and gets me in the flow of things. I watch television occasionally, and I get on my computer and I get lost in there. I read. I think there are many escapes that you can put yourself into. I love to go to the movies. There are things you can take to help you relax. There are certain foods that pacify you, like a dish of ice cream at night, which is always relaxing and delicious and dangerous, because a lot of people drown their depression or their stress in food. That's the big escape for a lot of us today – and the television, of course.

Janice: Why do parents have their favorite child, and then won't admit it?

Well some children are just more loveable than others. We are all unique and different, and in one family you can have five or six children, and they can all be totally different. I remember when I came from the hospital with my daughter, my first child, my brother-in- law said to my husband, "Oh, I'm sorry you didn't get your son." And I thought, wait a minute, you have a fine little girl here.

Some children are more affectionate than others, some are more scheming and they know how to get what they want. I don't know whether I had a favorite with my children or not.

I love them all, so I was so thankful to have each one of them. I had difficult pregnancies. There were times when one pleased me more than the other one. And there were times when I was disappointed in one. And I know that in some families, I had a neighbor whose child they called "a bad seed." She was really bad; she ended up in an automobile accident at 16, drunk driving. But the other children were normal, happy, successful children – why the bad seed, I don't know?

Janice: What is the secret to being married more than twenty years; how do you maintain a monogamous relationship with a man?

I guess because I grew up seeing my mom and dad; they were happily married. My grandparents, my friend's parents were also. You were married for life and that was it. You made the commitment and come hell or high water, you worked it out. Sure we had our ups and downs. There were times when we argued or we were upset about something, but we made a commitment to each to never go to bed angry. If we had to stay up all night to work out what we were upset about, then we stayed up all night. We didn't do that very often – one or two nights in all those years. We agreed that we would not go to bed angry – "Never let the sun set on an argument." I think that's good advice for anybody. So it's important and I wanted my marriage to last, so did my husband. We had parents who were happily married for 50 years.

And I know in working with young people today, children today have trouble making a commitment because they don't see it in their parents. I think we learn from watching. And we have to set our own goals and own rules and commitments to our selves. I wish that young people, baby boomers today, that I work with, there are so many that don't understand what the word commitment means. It means when you say something you're going to do it. When I volunteer to do something, I do it or I feel horrible if I don't. If I say I'm going to be somewhere on time, I get there early most of the time because I'm so afraid. Because I said 7:00, I'll be there at 7:00. I wish young people were brought up being told that when you say you're going to do something, you do it. If you have to bend over backwards, you do it and don't let other people down.

I forgot something one day and it took me weeks to get over it. I missed a luncheon – I totally forgot about it. I apologized, I sent her a gift, and I took her out to lunch. I felt terrible and yet I see it all the time with these young people. They don't show up for a meeting, they say, "I had something else to do." I'm thinking, well then change it or let the person know you're not going to be there - don't just don't show up, it's very rude.

Janice: How do parents instill the morals and values to their children that you were reared with?

Set a good example for your children. I think setting a good example is important - and talking with them and setting up rules and finding out what their goals are.

Janice: And the last question is, "What would you like to tell me that I didn't ask?"

What would I like most that maybe I don't have maybe in my life? I would like a little more financial freedom. I'd like to show off a $10,000 check to prove that I can do it.

Janice: Thank you so much for giving me your time and your wisdom.

I don't know how much wisdom! Thank you for asking me.

Lessons from Jodale

It's important to get a clear picture of what you want.

I've got one big goal that I am working on and if I keep being positive about it, not giving up, then I feel I will have it happen. I feel I have accomplished a lot of things in my life. I've set goals for years, I've been treasure-mapping, I put pictures on a large piece of paper. The pictures are of things I want in my life. I've got most everything I've put on my map. It's beautiful that you can create your future with pictures and affirmations and things like that.

Mediating on what you want helps you to
manifest it in your life.

I would also encourage [girls] to take time to be still and incorporate time for meditation everyday. Be still and go within and find that source. I used to say that meditating was the bottom line and it's what brought everything together . . . My son, when he was in college said, "Mom I just never have any time to do anything." And I said Pete; if you would take time to meditate you would have more time. He had trouble grasping that. But when he began to meditate, he realized that if he took time to be still and contemplate what he needed he managed to fit everything in.

. . . you just have to work at it, go within and pull from the source of strength that is within you.

You are a very special part of Creation.

Everybody is special and you are connected to a source you cannot be separated from, the energy of God. You're like a fish in the ocean - you're in it, you breathe it, you drink it, you can't be separated from it, you are part of it, wherever you are.

Learn to keep your word.

. . . young people don't understand what the word commitment means. It means when you say something, you're going to do it. When I volunteer to do something, I do it or I feel horrible if I don't. . . . I wish young people were brought up being told that when you say you're going to do something, you do it. If you have to bend over backwards you do it and don't let other people down. . . . I forgot something one day and it took me weeks to get over it. I apologized, I sent her a gift, and I took her out to lunch. I felt terrible, and yet I see it all the time with these young people. They don't show up for a meeting, they say, "I had something else to do." I'm thinking, well then change it or let the person know you're not going to be there. But just don't show up, it's very rude.

*Some decisions you make in life can come
back to haunt you.*

I think these young girls that go out and have sex at 12 and 14 years old, they are literally destroying their lives. Sex can beautiful with somebody that you truly love. . . It breaks my heart because many of them are getting all kinds of diseases, and they have to live with those things all the rest of their lives. And if they have an abortion, they have to live with that for the rest of their lives. All those things that happen when you're young never go away; they are there in your mind. You can bring them back and just relive them; even if it was fifty years ago, you still feel the emotions from that experience. I would hope that they would wait until they are really mentally prepared.

Discussion

1. **Why is it important to have a clear picture of what you want?**

   A. How can you become clear on what you want?

   B. Have you ever heard the expression, "I don't know what I want but I'll know it when I see it?"

   C. How does that phenomenon work?

2. **Gather together all the magazines that you can find.**

   A. Cut out pictures that represent a goal that you want to achieve in your life.

   B. Organize the pictures in to categories: mind, body, career, family, society, spirituality, significant others.

   C. Paste your pictures on the poster board and be prepared to discuss them with the group.

   D. How can you progress toward your goals and make some of these pictures become reality?

   E. Does having a picture of your goals help make them more real?

3 . **Define your spiritual beliefs.**

    A. Do you believe in a Supreme Being?

    B. How would you describe your spiritual self?

    C. Is it important that everyone have the same beliefs?

    D. Is it important to respectful of the beliefs of others?

4 . **How do you feel when someone breaks a promise to you?**

    A. How many times to you think you've broken promises?

    B. Why is it important to keep your word?

    C. How do you feel about people who don't keep their word?

    D. How can you make sure that you keep your word?

5 . **What is a consequence?**

    A. Is there a consequence associated with every action?

    B. Are all consequences bad?

    C. What are some of the consequences you've had to endure based on your previous actions?

    D. How can you begin to have more positive consequences?

6 . **What did you learn from Jodale?**

    A. What did you like about her?

    B. What didn't you like?

    C. Was there anything you didn't understand in her interview?

    D. Is there anything that you'd ask her for clarification or concerning a topic not covered in the interview?

Write a message to Jodale in 100 words or less.

We are born to manifest the glory of God that is within us. It's not just in some of us, it's in everyone.

- Nelson Mandela

Mattie Todd
The Caregiver

I met Ms. Todd when I was in junior high school. The occasion was my sister's wedding, almost 30 years ago. My sister married Ms. Todd's son. Over the years I've come to know her, when the families came together for various events like holidays, recitals, graduations, debutante balls and so forth. I think I was a little apprehensive about the interview because I knew she had a lot of wisdom to share and I wanted to make sure I got it exactly right. I wanted it to be an interview she was pleased with, so I would still be able to get a piece of her wonderful sweet potato pie.

It didn't take long to get over my fears. The interview turned out to be a very different interview. It was a more relaxed and informal interview. I have always known Ms. Todd to be an extremely caring person. We watched as she took care of her sick mother, and now she is expertly caring for her father. She has dedicated her life to making sure that those she loves get the best possible care. Ms. Todd is one of those grandmothers that always has some type of goodie waiting for you when you come by. I have eaten a many of wonderful meals at her table. Therefore, she was on my original list of wonderful women that I wanted to interview for this project.

Ms. Todd raised a very successful son, who in turn has raised two beautiful and successful daughters. So I knew there had to be successes to share with the girls I was working with. Ms. Todd has a quiet and easy spirit, and does not often talk about herself. She is usually too busy caring for others, so it was a special treat to sit down and talk to her and learn about her life, her goals, her joys and sorrows and have her give advice to my girls. Her interview is short, but packed with wisdom, kindness and caring.

Mattie Todd

Mattie...

My name is Mattie Bell Todd. I am originally from Alabama. My birthday is March 12, 1928. I grew up on a plantation farm; my grandfather sharecropped. I learned how to pick cotton, chop cotton, pull corn, chip a cane and pick up sweet potatoes. We'd have to get up early in the morning and milk the cows before we'd go to the field. And usually we were in the field at about 6:30 or 7:00 in the morning. And my mother was one of the persons that worked in the white people's house. I worked on the farm and raised chickens. We had goats and we used to have guineas. This generation wouldn't know about that. That's what we would have for Sunday dinner, Guineas and dressing. We went to school in a one-room church building, and that school went from elementary preschool to sixth grade. And after we finished the sixth grade, we had to move away to go to high school, it started in seventh grade. I lived with Mrs. Francis on weekdays and on Fridays I would go home. Sometimes we walked about thirteen miles from Ms. Francis' to my home. A bunch of us would get in a row; it was fun and we'd walk home. And Mondays we'd go back. There was a bus that came from Montgomery to Selma, so we would ride the bus on Monday morning. The bus fare was only 25 cents at the time.

And when we got home from school, we had to go to the pump. You had to pour water into the pump in order to get water - prime it. That was our chores and we would have to cook for the old lady. And we would sit down at night and she would tell us things that we should and should not do in life.

Janice: You remember any of those stories?

Well it wasn't really stories; she was just telling you how to live and how to treat people. I remember very well she used to tell me, "Baby, a still tongue carries a wise head - the less you talk, the better off you'll be." "Always treat people nice, and feed them with a long handled spoon" I wondered what did she mean by feeding people with a long handled spoon. But that's just don't tell them all of your business, that's what she really meant. She used to tell you how to cook. We had to make a fire in the fire place. My father would bring us wood to have fire in the fire place. And we often would sit around the fireplace at night and eat peanuts, and it was just wonderful. There were several girls that boarded with this lady, but somehow she'd always call me her baby. I was always the youngest in my group. And she'd always say "Baby, be smart and keep your house clean." And now since I've gotten older, I've tried to dwell on more things that she used to say.

So after graduating from high school, my first year home, Mrs. Francis passed away. After leaving school, I came to Birmingham and I lived with my Aunt. Later, momma and daddy moved here, and we decided, we'd just all come here, and that's been over fifty years ago. After we moved to Birmingham, Daddy bought a little house down near Shield School. After our children were born, Mike and Sadie, they were so fortunate they lived right across the street from the school. And in the late seventies, the I-65 highway came through, and we moved to this present place. My children went to Hayes High School, and from there to Alabama A & M University in Huntsville. We were members of a small church which we loved very much.

I grew up an only child. My mother and daddy had two children, but I had a sister who was a year and eight months younger than me, who passed away. After that my mother wanted another little girl. And she tried her best to get a cousin of ours. Back then they didn't call it adopting a baby, they called it "handwriting," but her parents wouldn't give her away. They would often let her come stay with us, but I grew up an only child and I had one child, Michael. He was very smart in school, and for some reason, everybody just loved him. He started in kindergarten at about three years old. He was always the head of his class through high school. I remember very well, this church that we belonged to, we had conventions once a year. When Michael was a teenager, he would walk in the church and say one or two words, and people would just shout and fall out over him. And they would give him money for just saying two words. He's always been a smart child. (laughter) At one point in his life he was stricken with asthma, and he went through about six years in and out of the hospital. But prayer brought him through. Everybody prayed for him. My aunt Bessie and the Saints would get together in the middle of the day and have prayer meeting for him. People would tell him "You look like a preacher," and he would teach Sunday school. My Mother thought Michael was straight out of heaven. I'm sure everybody else did, and I did too. People from the church and our neighbors would say, "That boy is going places in life." There was just something about him, from a child on up. When he was a little, little fella, he would put his arms around my neck. I said, "Michael, are you going to always love me?" And he said "My Belle, I will always love you." He called me "My Belle." But he was crazy about my mother. And Momma would spoil him too. They just took Michael. They said I could go anywhere I wanted to go, but Michael was going to be their child. I had wonderful parents and I have a wonderful son.

Janice: What do you consider to be the best invention of your lifetime?

Well living in the computer age is great. And the telephone was quite an invention. I guess I was about 17 years old when we first received a radio. But I think the telephone and the computer are the greatest.

Janice: Is there anything that was invented that you wished had never been invented?

No.

Janice: What do you consider to be your life's greatest joy?

My grandchildren are my greatest joy. My grandchildren have been a great tremendous joy. And I can't explain how I felt the day I saw my granddaughter, Tania, receive her college degree. I wanted to see them educated and know they didn't have to work in the cotton fields or clean up white people's houses like I did. So far, this has been one of my greatest joys – my grandchildren.

Janice: What do you consider to be your life's greatest sorrow?

Well, the greatest sorrow I've had in my life is my mother having Alzheimer's. And my father lost his leg. I can't explain to you, what I went through at that time. My father is 93. I consider this a blessing, yes, but I hate to see him suffer. But God is able and he seems to accept his disability.

Janice: When you look back over your life, is there something that you regret not having done, or something that you did do that you regret?

I regret that I didn't further my education. I finished high school but I didn't go on.

Janice: How has the position and value of women changed over your lifetime?

Well, the position for women has changed. In my day, we didn't have as many women in the political world as we do now. And even in the churches, years ago women didn't have a voice. But now we have women leaders, we have women ministers and teachers. I think women have made great progress within the last 30 years.

Janice: Do you believe it was easier to be a girl when you were a girl, or do you believe it is easier to be a girl now?

I actually think it was easier being a girl when I was a girl. We didn't hear of all the disaster that we hear about now. But now when young girls are out, you're worried. There is more danger for them now than when I was a girl. I think its easier being a girl back in my day than it is now.

Janice: Do you think it's important for a woman to have a husband or boyfriend in her life?

Yes, because male and female belong together. I think it's important for a woman to have a husband or a boyfriend in her life. But I don't think girls should put the boyfriend first. Falling in love is all right. You're supposed to love who you want to love. But don't love so much that you forget about your goals. I think all women should accomplish goals in their life., but it's nice to love and be loved. But sometimes girls focus so much on finding a boyfriend and getting married that they lose sight of their goals and the other important things in her life. I think a girl's first priority should be to accomplish her goals. But yet, I still feel like male and female belong together, if it is not an abusive relationship. Falling in love is all right. You're supposed to love who you want to love. But don't be so in love that you forget about your goals. It's nice to love and be loved.

Janice: This is a three-part question. What one thing do you wish women understood about life? About love? Longevity?

When it comes to love, don't lose your mind over love. It's nice to be sociable; it's nice to be in love. Most young people fall in love and after they grow older they realize that who they have fallen in love with has serious faults. So I would say be sure you know who you're falling in love with. Don't just fall in love with anybody out there. Within your heart, nine times out of ten, you will know when the right person

for you comes along. Don't be fooled, and don't let nobody
abuse you because, they say, "I love you." Don't ignore your
feelings; when you heart tells you something might be
wrong, listen to your heart.

Janice: What is your secret to longevity?

Well, I don't know because I haven't done anything out of
the ordinary, except ask God for blessings.

**Janice: What do you consider to be your recipe for a fulfilling
life?**

What makes life fulfilling for me is doing for people, I love
people. And anything that I can do for anybody, I'm willing
to do it. And if I feel like I've mistreated anybody, I'm not
too big to tell you I'm sorry. I love my neighbors as myself.
And anything I can do to help somebody, I want to do

**Janice: What do you consider to be the best advice that
anybody ever gave you?**

Live by the Golden Rule.

**Janice: As you look back over your life, is there anything that
you know now at age 73 that you wished you had known
twenty years ago, thirty years ago or forty years ago?**

Well like I said, I wished that I had not given up on going to
school. And I think I've done pretty much what I've wanted
to do. I've had decent jobs, lovely friends. So looking back

on my life, my biggest regret is that I didn't further my education. That's my largest regret of life.

Janice: Imagine that you have a 14 year old daughter and you were going to have to leave her alone. What advice would you give her to help her succeed?

I would tell her as I do say now, "Get all the education that you can get, and in all of your getting, don't forget the bridge that has brought you across, because you might have to cross that bridge again. Go as far in school as you can go."

Janice: You have raised a very successful son. What do you consider to be the best way to raise children?

The best way to raise children would be to live with them. When I say that, don't be too busy for your child. I remember when Michael was a child he loved football all of his life, and I would sit down with him, and he was teaching me how to play football when he was a little fellow. Find time for your children; don't be too busy for your children. Listen to them, even if what they are telling you isn't interesting. Find a way to share with them, become interested in what they are interested in. Find time to be together. I don't believe in scolding my children, I like to sit down and reason with them. It's the communication that you have with your child that will make all the difference.

Janice: How do you motivate yourself to keep on going?

Well, like I said, I depend on God. I wake up in the morning and say "Lord I thank you for this day, and guide me through this day and let me be the legs for daddy and me and take care of my children."

Janice: What do you see as the solution for young people's plights - the things that young people go through, like drugs, alcohol, different diseases, dropping out of school?

Temptation is out there and it takes a strong child to fight these temptations. I think our churches have a big part to play in it. If you could just get your child to attend church and learn how to handle temptation. They can be easily tempted. If you could just get them in the Word or in the church, that would be a help. Some churches do have a lot of activities for young people. The main thing is to be involved in their lives, talk to them, get involved in things that interest them and keep them in school - make sure they don't have too much idle time. I think the parents being there with the child and guiding them is the key to solving many of their problems.

Janice: Tell me a little bit about what your daily routine is like?

It's pretty busy. I get up and I water my flowers; usually, I have flowers in the summer. If my daddy is still sleeping, I'll make coffee and start breakfast. So when he gets up I help him get cleaned up and get his clothes on. And by the time I get him straightened out, then I make sure he eats breakfast. Next, I do the laundry; I wash every day. By the time I get through with that, it's time to fix lunch. And after lunch, I have one soap opera that I watch. And I do spend a lot of time on the telephone. Next it's time to do dinner, and after dinner I'm back on the telephone again. Then my day is gone. Every morning I get up with the same routine: cooking and washing and sweeping the floor - routine housework.

Janice: What should you do when your mother does not want to be a mother and she does not protect you?

Well, I really don't know because that's a bad feeling for your mother not to want you. I think she should find a teacher, a minister or whoever that she can talk to for advice. I would hate to have my mother reject me.

Janice: The next question comes from the same little girl. She says, "How do you stay hopeful in a world that is hopeless?"

Stay in prayer. The only way you can stay hopeful is through prayer.

Janice: At what age did you fall in love and how did you know it was love that you felt?

There's not a sure way of knowing who loves you, but you can pretty much tell if a person loves you by how much time he spends with you or how he treats you. I think you should be a little older than 15 to be thinking about love. Don't be in a hurry. As you get a little older you'll realize there is a difference between what you felt as a teenager and a more mature love. You can go out and get a boyfriend at anytime.

Janice: And what age would you advise me to get married?

Between 25 and 30. Try to accomplish your goals before you get married. That's what I think a girl should do.

Janice: My mother and I have not been close, but I'd like to open up to her and share my feelings, how should I do that?

Well, sometimes you have to reach out. And sometimes if you open up to her maybe she will stop and listen. And as mothers get older, they will understand their children better. And she will listen to them.

Janice: How do you cope with the loss of a loved one?

Well you realize if you've lost a parent, you know life has to go on and you just have to learn to pray and fellowship with other people and talk. Get out and associate with other people. I don't think any mother or father would want their child just sitting down moaning all the time. Just realize life has to go on.

Janice: What advice would you give a single mother raising children?

There is only one thing you can do, make sure they know where you stand. Be clear when you tell them what is and is not acceptable.   Always have time for your child, talk to them and encourage them to do the right thing is all situations.   Encourage them to get interested in athletics. Playing sports helps children learn about life, working with other people and accomplishing goals. Talk to your child's counselors and teachers and make sure you work with them to make your child the best he/she can be.

Janice: How have you dealt with racism in America?

Well, at my age, we went through a period of segregation. But all my life I worked with white people, and I dealt with them real well during my lifetime. You don't want anyone to know too much about your life, because white folks don't care nothing about us. I don't care how they smile at you, they don't care for us. Even at this day and time, they'll walk with you, you can sit and eat with them, but some of them are not to be trusted.

Janice: Do you feel you got a chance to finish all of your life's goals?

Well I have some that I would like to accomplish, but at this stage of the game I don't know if I'll be able to. I'd like to have a new house and a new car.

Janice: What do you think is the biggest mistake that young women in this age make about love?

Not being independent. If you were independent you can take care of yourself. Don't let love overpower your good senses. You can love someone and still look out for yourself.

Janice: Why is that you think that teenagers don't listen to their parents?

Teenagers don't listen to their parents too much because you get to an age where you think your parents don't know anything. I guess it's pretty much been this way now through the years. Rearing a child is not easy.

Janice: How has getting older changed your viewpoints on things?

Well getting older changes your viewpoints on things because you know you have missed so many things in life, things such as traveling and furthering your education in school. You think, well I guess I'm just a little too old for that now.

Janice: If you had to do it all over again - we're going to move you back to March 1928 and start you all over again.

I don't particularly know anything that I would want to do over again. As I look back on my life, I think I just live it day by day. I don't particularly know anything that I would like to redo - except get more education.

Janice: How can I show my mother that I'm very responsible so that I can get out of the house more?

Well behave yourself! (laughter) Show her that you're all grown up now; you're a young adult that you can take care of yourself. And then you'll learn that there is not too much out on the street anyway. Show your parents that you are independent and responsible.

Janice: As a legacy, what would you like to leave behind for your children and grandchildren?

I just want them to know that I love them, that they were the joys of my life and I enjoy them. And when I'm gone, I want everyone to know that Belle loved them. That's all I can leave them is love and trust in God.

Janice: Do you have any quotes that you would share with them?

I just hope they go on and get the education that I didn't get. By all means be independent, I don't care how much you love a husband or wife, they might get tired and walk off. Be where you can do for yourself. I've instilled that in the grandchildren - be where you can take care of yourself. And my momma used to often tell me, "Whatever you do, keep a nickel for yourself. Momma may have, poppa may have, but God bless that child that has his own." So that's the biggest advice that I can give. Prepare yourself to be independent, and by all means, depend on God.

Janice: I thank you immensely for taking the time to be interviewed.

Lessons from Mattie

Be careful what you say.

"Baby, a still tongue carries a wise head, the less you talk the better off you'll be."

Try not to lose you in love.

I think it's important for a woman to have a husband or a boyfriend in her life. But, I don't think girls should put the boyfriend first. Falling in love is all right. You're supposed to love, who you want to love. But don't love so much that you forget about your goals . . . sometimes, girls focus so much on finding a boyfriend and getting married that they lose sight of their goals and the other important things in her life. I think a girl's first priority should be to accomplish her goals.

There are a few tale tale signs to indicate if someone really loves you.

There's not a sure way of knowing who loves you but you can pretty much tell if a person loves you by how much time he spends with you or how he treats you. . . . Don't be in a hurry. As you get a little older you'll realize there is a difference between what you felt as a teenager and a more mature love.

Self Preservation is the first law of nature.

[The biggest mistake girls make in love is] not being independent. If you were independent you can take care of yourself. Don't let love overpower your good senses. You can love someone and still look out for yourself. . . . By all means be independent, I don't care how much you love a husband or wife, they might get tired and walk off. Be where you can do for yourself . . . be where you can take care of yourself. "Whatever you do, keep a nickel for yourself. Momma may have, poppa may have, but God bless that child that has his own."

If you want more freedom, then be more responsible.

[If you want to get out more and not be treated like a child] well behave yourself! Show (your parents) that you're all grown up now; you're a young adult that you can take care of yourself. Show your parents that you are independent and responsible.

FAVORITE BOOK

The Bible

Discussion

1. **How might the words you say get you in trouble?**

   A. Have you ever said something that you had to try to take back?

   B. How easy was it to take it back?

   C. Have you ever been quoted out of context?

   D. Have you ever said something that you thought was in confidence and found out it was repeated?

   E. How can you avoid that happening?

2. **Has there ever been a time when you put someone else's wants and needs above your own?**

   A. What was the outcome of that situation?

   B. Did the other person ever reciprocate?

   C. How did it make you feel?

   D. Who had the advantage in that situation?

   E. Do you regret putting someone else's needs above your own?

   F. Does doing so, make the person love or respect you more?

3 . If someone loves you, how do you really know?

A. Make a list of indicators that someone loves you?

B. Make a list of the things you do if you really love someone?

C. What are the things that are in common on the two lists?

D. What do you do if someone who you thought loved you doesn't do any of the things that are on either list?

E. Do their actions have any reflections on their feelings?

F. What actions should give you an indication that someone does not love you, because of the way they treat you?

4 . How can you balance loving someone yourself and someone else?

A. In what says can you lose yourself in a relationship?

B. What are the signs that a girl has lost herself, because of a relationship?

C. What should you do if you see it happening to a friend?

D. What should you do if you feel it's happening to you?

E. How can you avoid it happening to you?

F. Make a list of the ways you can make sure you have a balanced relationship?

5 . **Why do you feel that parents want to limit the freedoms their teenagers have?**

A. Have you ever betrayed your parents trust?

B. What were the circumstances?

C. How did it make your parents feel?

D. How did you feel?

E. Has your parents treating you like a child ever been justified?

F. What actions should a responsible teenager take?

6 . **What did you learn from Mattie?**

A. What did you like about her?

B. What didn't you like?

C. Was there anything you didn't understand?

D. Is there anything you'd ask her for clarification or concerning a topic not covered in the interview?

E. Are there any points that you disagree with her own?

Write a message to Mattie in 100 words or less.

www.ingramcontent.com/pod-product-compliance
Lightning Source LLC
Chambersburg PA
CBHW031829090426
42741CB00005B/180